Davenport's Illinois Wills and Estate Planning Legal Forms

DAVENPORT'S ILLINOIS WILLS AND ESTATE PLANNING LEGAL FORMS

written by attorneys
Alex Russell and Robert Maxwell

**BOOK AND FORMS FREE AT
WWW.DAVENPORTPUBLISHING.COM**

COPYRIGHT © 2022 -- ALEX RUSSELL AND ROBERT MAXWELL

CREATIVE COMMONS LICENSE. This work is also licensed under a Creative Commons Attribution-NonCommercial-NoDerivatives 4.0 International License.

GOVERNMENT WORKS. No claim is made to copyright or ownership of government materials.

SOME STANDARD FORMS. No copyright or ownership is claimed of "standard" forms or leading forms for the state which are provided in this book, but fair use and privilege to use is claimed. Makers of such forms (often a state agency or hospital) have agreed by word, action, inaction, and implication forms may be used and copied if no profit is sought and no substantial changes made. Such makers if not a lawyer or law firm are barred from profit or advantage by practicing law to make legal forms then limit use. Authors believe in a religious and legal duty to help people.

PUBLICATION DATA
(informal, library may use different data)

Names: Russell, Alex, 1972- author ; Maxwell, Robert, 1960- author

Title: Davenport's Illinois Wills And Estate Planning Legal Forms

Other Titles: Davenport's Wills

Description: Davenport Publishing 2022

Suggested Other Identifiers: 9798365810211, LCCN 2021909030, 9798748423373

Subjects: LCSH: Wills--United States;
                       Wills--United States--Forms;
                       Estate Planning--United States;
                       Legal Forms

Classification: LFF KF755 .C55 2022 (or as library chooses)
                       DDC 346.73 Rus--dc23 (or as library chooses)

9 8 7 6 5 4 3 2 1 0 0 0 0 0 2 3

PERMISSION TO COPY AND USE BOOKS FOR FREE

To help people and groups publisher and authors of the book allow mostly free use by giving all a "Creative Commons Attribution-NonCommercial-NoDerivatives 4.0 International License". Most users face no limit on copying, using, holding in library to loan out, or giving out copies.

Basically, as the image below says, any copying or use is OK if it still shows it is by the authors, is non-commercial (nc) with no price charged, and has no derivatives (nd) so no big changes.

(This work licensed under a Creative Commons Attribution-NonCommercial-NoDerivatives 4.0 International License.)

TO GET COPIES OF BOOKS USE WWW.DAVENPORTPUBLISHING.COM OR AMAZON.COM.

EMAIL ANY QUESTIONS TO DAVENPORTPRESS@GMAIL.COM.

WARNING

THIS PUBLICATION IS NOT A SUBSTITUTE FOR LEGAL ADVICE. Publisher and authors say and warn this publication is not giving any legal, accounting, or other professional services or advice, which if wanted can be obtained by consulting in person an attorney or some other professional. **No attorney-client relationship or any relationship creating a duty or obligation is agreed to or created by the purchase or use of this publication or forms.**

BOOKS AND FORMS FOR OTHER STATES ARE AVAILABLE, SEE WWW.DAVENPORTPUBLISHING.COM FOR INFORMATION

CHAPTER	TABLE OF CONTENTS	PAGE NUMBER
1 -	BOOK BASICS AND LIST OF FORMS	1
2 -	LEGAL TERMS, PROPERTY, HELPFUL INFORMATION FORM	3
3 -	WILL BASICS	8
4 -	WILL GIFTS INCLUDING RESIDUE	10
5 -	DEBT, MARRIAGE, AND YOUNG CHILD ISSUES	14
6 -	BASIC IDEAS ABOUT HEALTH CARE FORMS	17

AFTER DEATH FORMS

7 -	FORM 1: WILL (STANDARD)	18
8 -	FORM 2: WILL (GUARDIANS)	22
9 -	FORM 3: SELF-PROVING AFFIDAVIT	26

HEALTH CARE FORMS

10 -	FORM 4: STATUTORY SHORT FORM POWER OF ATTORNEY FOR HEALTH CARE	28
11 -	FORM 5: LIVING WILL DECLARATION	35
12 -	FORM 6: DO-NOT-RESUSCITATE	37

GIVING POWER FORMS

13 -	FORM 7: STATUTORY SHORT FORM POWER OF ATTORNEY FOR PROPERTY	40
14 -	FORM 8: APPOINTMENT OF SHORT-TERM GUARDIAN (FOR MINOR CHILD)	49
15 -	FORM 9: APPOINTMENT OF AGENT TO CONTROL DISPOSITION OF REMAINS	53

APPENDIX:	HOW TO GET FORMS AND SAMPLE FILLED OUT FORMS	56

CHAPTER 1
BOOK BASICS AND LIST OF FORMS

ESTATE PLANNING CONTROLS THINGS IF LATER ABSENT, SICK, OR DEAD

From Davenport Publishing and written by attorneys this book is on "Estate Planning", about doing legal documents to control health care, property, money, children, funeral, and more if later absent, sick, or dead. People have a legal right to control their health care, property, money, and family issues, and so judges, doctors, and others mostly just ask: **"Based on what a person wrote what did they likely want done?"**

ESTATE PLANNING MOSTLY IS DOING SIMPLE THINGS IN 3 AREAS

Estate Planning is mostly doing simple things in 3 areas: After Death, Health Care, and Giving Power. There are 9 legal forms for Illinois in this book. Many people use just 2 to 4 of these legal forms.

AFTER DEATH FORMS

Form 1. Will (Standard) – lets person control some things after death especially gifts of property and money, and this Form 1 is the most used Will in this book and suits most people.

Form 2. Will (Guardians) – this is Will with parts added to name a "Guardian" to if needed care for any minor child under 18, and also person to care for their estate and property.

Form 3. Self-Proving Affidavit – this form can help with later work of showing Will was properly signed.

HEALTH CARE FORMS

Form 4. Statutory Short Form Power Of Attorney For Health Care – this is often the only health care form done and it lets a person be named "Health Care Agent" to if needed control health care and form also lets health care instructions be written.

Form 5. Living Will Declaration – this form does extreme act of in writing refusing most further health care if later doctors determine health situation has gotten very bad and more care likely won't help.

Form 6. Do-Not-Resuscitate – does extreme act of saying from now on do not give certain health care including C.P.R., and does this in short 2 pages to be read fast and usually by paramedics outside a facility.

GIVING POWER FORMS

Form 7. Statutory Short Form Power Of Attorney For Property – lets power over money, property, and more be shared during life with "Agent" who often is spouse, family, or friend so they can help do things.

Form 8. Appointment Of Short-Term Guardian (For Minor Child) – lets parent or similar with child under 18 share power over child's health care, schooling, discipline, home, and more with person named as "Guardian" so they can help control things if needed (like if parent is away for weeks or often from child).

Form 9. Appointment Of Agent To Control Disposition Of Remains – lets instructions be written and person named to control funeral and bodily remains (instead of following law that closest family does this).

ILLINOIS ESTATE PLANNING LAW APPLIES TO MOST PEOPLE HERE
This book is for Illinois only. The law and legal documents can be very different in different states. Whether local Estate Planning law applies is based on primary residence of a person (sometimes called "domicile"). Many judges say residence occurs when a person lives in a place with no definite plans to leave. Later plans to move don't matter till people move. People can stay under a state's Estate Planning laws even if they leave if any living elsewhere is temporary and people keep firm plans to return. For example some people who leave months or more for travel, for school, for special work projects, and for the military may qualify to keep ties to their old state. Immigrants of any kind usually can do normal Estate Planning. For health care people often do legal documents to match the state that a hospital or other facility is in.

BOOK IS SHORT, HAS FORMS TO QUICKLY SEE, AND USES EMPHASIS
This book is short and may read rough but can be read quickly. Long books tend to lead to skimming and misunderstanding. The book has many legal forms people can quickly see. For emphasis paragraph titles, underlining, and boxes are used. This book capitalizes words like Will, Testator, and Agent but this is optional. To save space some small words are skipped and end quotation marks put before punctuation.

LEGAL FORMS CAN HELP AND THIS BOOK PROVIDES "STANDARD FORMS"
Estate Planning research shows a surprising 60% of people die without doing anything, 19% use a lawyer, and 21% use legal forms. Legal forms are good at most things involved in Estate Planning and can make binding legal documents that judges, doctors, families, banks, and others legally must follow. Also, often a hospital, state agency, charity, or state legislature has made a form most people use and call the "standard form", and doctors, judges, and others may not like to follow different forms. This book does use a standard form in an area if it exists or provides a suitable form. Lawyers often write their own forms.

THIS BOOK COVERS MAJOR IDEAS AND SHOULD SUIT MOST PEOPLE
This book covers the main U.S. legal ideas on Estate Planning and most major ways Illinois law is a bit different. This book and its forms can't cover every issue that matters to everyone but should suit people without strange situations or wishes about Estate Planning, which is maybe most people (maybe over 90%). Strange situations or wishes that may need more research or a lawyer include: a) unusual wishes for gifts, b) wealth over $3 million, c) big medical concerns in family, d) property or money going to a person with disability or special needs, and e) wish to hide or move assets to quickly qualify for government programs. People after reading this book can do more research or talk to a lawyer if they want.

ESTATE PLANNING OFTEN IS NOT THAT IMPORTANT
Estate Planning is often not vital and worth much time or money, and may not affect costs, delays, work, and other things as much as thought. For young adults and parents the benefits seem low since only about 9% of people die by 60, and only about 0.13% of children under 18 had 2 parents die to likely need help. *Social Security Tables: Felicitie Bell*; *Census Life Factors Mortality Study #288*. A lawyer can be used for Estate Planning but they can cost $1000s, take months of work, and make mistakes. In life people weigh costs, benefits, and risks and often go with a low cost option. Many people to try to help their family more buy life insurance ($100,000 of term life by just questionnaire ("simplified issue") is about $500/year).

CHAPTER 2
LEGAL TERMS, PROPERTY, HELPFUL INFORMATION FORM

THERE ARE BASIC TERMS AND IDEAS IN WILLS AND ESTATE PLANNING

Some legal terms and ideas are basic to Wills and Estate Planning.

■ "Estate Planning" is people doing legal documents to control things if later absent, sick, or dead. After a document is signed people are usually still free to sell or transfer property, instruct doctors, or change forms.

■ A "person doing a legal document" and "doing a form" means the form is for and affects that person.

■ A "Will" or "will" (this book uses upper case "W") is a legal document done to control issues after death. The phrase "Last Will And Testament" is used since a "Testament" long ago was a small document done along with a Will to do some things. If no Will is done a person is described as being "intestate".

■ A person who died is called "decedent" or "deceased". A person getting money or property can be called "recipient", "beneficiary", or if related "heir" (they "inherit"). "Survive" or "surviving" is being alive after a death.

■ Someone picked by a person to do things after their death is called by most people the "Executor".

■ A person doing a Will is called "Testator" or "Will maker". Before about 1990 a woman Testator was called a "Testatrix" and woman Executor called an "Executrix" but this is no longer often done.

■ "Probate" is a legal process to do things after death like transfer property, authorize a Guardian, and handle creditors. Due to nice changes in law probate is now often "informal", faster, and less expensive.

■ The "estate" is both a) all property and money of person that at their death did not automatically transfer to other owners, and b) the entity run by an Executor several months to hold items and do things (sort of like a small corporation). For example accounts may be renamed, like: "Estate of John Smith (deceased)".

■ Property is: 1) "real property" (land and buildings), 2) "fixtures" (things tied to real property like fences and wired-in appliances), or 3) "personal property" (everything else like clothes, cars, cash, and investments).

■ Legal documents to control health care things are often called "Advanced Directives", but names vary.

■ In Illinois a person under 18 is called a "minor" and a parent or "Guardian" mostly handles their affairs. A minor or other person not reasonably able to make wise decisions lacks "capacity" and is "incapacitated".

■ Forms giving power to someone are often called "Power of Attorney" forms. The person giving power is called the "Principal" and person getting power is called the "Attorney-in-Fact" or "Agent".

■ State law is the "Illinois Compiled Statutes" (the "ILCS"), with dozens of big "Chapters". For example, a law in Chapter 25 might look like "25 ILCS 135/5.04". A law is usually called a "statute" or "section" (often shown by "§" or "s"). A form put in statues by legislature for people to use if wanted is a "statutory form".

LEGAL DOCUMENTS MAY NEED TO BE "WITNESSED" OR "NOTARIZED"

Legal documents to be valid may need to be "witnessed", which is someone acting as witness watching person doing form sign and then witness signs. Documents may need to be "notarized", which is person who is a "notary" (also called "notary public") see signing and use ink stamp on page and then notary signs too. Notaries are found at some banks, brokers, insurance agents, courts, and government offices but they are often busy or just help current customers. <u>A helpful notary often can be found using a phonebook and calling</u>.

ANYONE CAN FILL IN MOST OF A FORM, AND LATER TRY TO KEEP ORIGINAL

When filling out a form <u>except for certain special forms and except for signatures</u> other parts can be filled in by a person not doing the form for themselves. After a legal form is completed and signed usually people try to keep the original and hand out copies but situations vary. Some people do "multiple originals" by having everyone sign identical documents to have many pages with real ink signatures but this can be confusing.

PROBABLY DO NEW FORMS IF DIVORCE, MARRY, HAVE CHILD, OR MOVE

Divorcing, marrying, birth or adoption of child, or moving to a new state can have major legal effects. If any of these events occur it is recommended people do a new Will and other Estate Planning papers soon. To help most states say a Will from another state is still valid but this is not always certain.

"INTESTATE" LAW SAYS WHERE THINGS GO AT DEATH IF THERE IS NO WILL

State "intestate law" says where a dead person's property and money goes if no valid Will was done (except for certain rights of spouses, family, and creditors). This often says half and sometimes all goes (in order) to any spouse, half or any remainder to decedent's children natural or adopted, then next close family, and then the state. <u>Some people are happy with how intestate law would transfer things and skip a Will</u>.

NO FEDERAL OR ILLINOIS TAX IS USUALLY OWED AT A DEATH

Usually no tax is owed as a result of a death, including no estate, inheritance, death, or similar taxes. This is since the "Federal Estate And Gift Tax" only starts when a tax credit is used up covering <u>$13.99 million per person in 2025 and later</u>. Illinois has an Estate Tax but it only applies if a person died with over $4 million of money or property (this tax use to be worse and started at just $1 million in 2011).

PEOPLE SHOULD DETERMINE WHAT THEY OWN SO CAN GIVE AWAY

A person can only gift by Will and other ways things they own so <u>people should research what they own</u>. Property law says a person usually owns all they earn as wages and salary, their share of income and profit tied to property they own, and owns or partly owns any things their money or property buys or improves. For items with "title" documents (real estate or vehicles) or where there is a "listed owner" (like accounts and various investments) the named persons are often legal owners unless evidence shows special facts. A person during life can sell property, make gifts, or transfer things even if they are named in a Will, so <u>people should consider if they already sold or gave away property they name in a Will gift</u>.

THINGS OWNED IN SPECIAL WAYS MAY LIMIT GIFTING IN WILL

A person should consider if they own real estate or other property in special ways which may limit

gifting by Will. Laws in different states vary but some special joint ways are:
  a) "joint tenant with right of survivorship" or similar legal things, so then property transfers automatically to the other named owners regardless of a Will, which in some states is usually how the family house is held,
  b) papers say a "life estate" exists, so then if life of someone ends the other people in papers get item, and
  c) "Trust property" occurs if paperwork made a Trust entity and property was transferred into it, so then at or after a death the Trust papers tell a Trustee where to transfer such property.

Normal joint property for the part owned <u>can</u> be gifted by Will, like "I give my half of boat to Paul Lucas Fox". Joint ownership can come from agreement, paperwork, use of joint funds, or if a gift was to many people.

WARNING: "NON-PROBATE PROPERTY" TRANSFERS IGNORE ANY WILL

Money or property that for some reason automatically transfers on death or soon after to new owners is called "non-probate property". Examples of non-probate property are: a) if a "designated beneficiary" form was done to name persons to get account or investment, b) transfer-on-death account, and c) real estate like a house held by 2 people as "joint tenants with survivorship" or similar so survivor gets things. Insurance with a beneficiary usually ignores a Will. <u>Trying to do non-probate transfers for all things is called "avoiding probate"</u>, but it is rare as it may make living and paperwork a hassle for years, benefits are small, and it is hard to not miss an item and fail. <u>People should consider non-probate transfers that will occur automatically on death and consider what property and money will be left to transfer by Will.</u>

SOME LESS COMMON AND LESS USEFUL FORMS ARE NOT IN THIS BOOK

This book skips some less common or less useful documents.

1. A "Codicil" can modify a Will but it is easier and safer to just re-do a Will.

2. Illinois law unlike some states doesn't let a simple writing like a list or memo be done add gifts to a Will.

3. Some people do a "Revocable Living Trust" so Trust entity with Trustee holds property or money during their life however long, usually done to after death avoid small delay, costs, or work (by "avoiding probate"). This is rare as it requires immediately moving most of a person's things into a Trust causing maybe years of hassles, mostly for small benefits for people who are probably happy to later do work to get things by Will.

4. "Childrens Trust" papers can be done with a Will so a Trust upon a death gets a minor child's money or property to manage until 18, but this is uncommon due to possible cost and hassles, since it rarely matters (as this book shows), and since most Wills already arrange other help or a judge can do this if needed.

5. Some people do a "Pet Trust" to help a pet, but it's easier to just give money in Will to person given a pet.

6. Though separate forms exist most people handle any organ donation in drivers license or state ID forms.

7. Complex documents may be suggested for tax reasons but as this book shows taxes are rarely an issue.

"HELPFUL INFORMATION" FORM CAN TELL FAMILY AND FRIENDS THINGS

<u>People can do an unofficial "Helpful Information" form</u> banks, lawyers, and planners suggest so family or friends after a death will know things. People can staple records or lists to this. <u>See form on next pages</u>.

ESTATE PLANNING HELPFUL INFORMATION

For more space attach copies of form or blank pages. Keep pages by a Will or other place for Executor or family.

1. Personal Information (Name, Birthdate, Social Security number, special family details, other):

2. Real estate, vehicles, and other major tangible property (especially if people may not find them):

3. Non-tangible assets like stocks, accounts, investments, loans owed you, and business interests:

4. Possible income or insurance like pensions, retirement, disability, insurance, or contracts:

5. Debts owed by you like credit card, loan, student loan, mortgage, car loans, and accounts payable:

6. Names and information of professionals used (attorneys, accountants, brokers, doctors, others):

7. Computer passwords and helpful files, document places, and safes or safe-deposit boxes code/key:

8. Other helpful things, wishes for funeral, special requests, and last messages to family and friends:

CHAPTER 3
WILL BASICS

WILL LETS "TESTATOR" CONTROL SOME THINGS AFTER THEIR DEATH

A Will is legal document done by person to control some things after their death, like who gets money and property, who is Executor, who is Guardian for child, and to say some costs or delays can be avoided. To do Will a person must be at least 18 and <u>when signing</u> be of sound mind (rational with fair memory) and not under duress (illegal pressure or threat). A person doing a Will is called the "Testator" or "Will maker". The law usually requires gifts and other wishes for things to occur after a death be handled in a Will.

USUALLY SIGN WILL IN FRONT OF 2 WITNESSES WHO THEN SIGN

USUALLY A WILL TO BE VALID MUST BE WRITTEN AND HAVE 2 WITNESSES

Usually to be a valid Illinois Will it must a) show it is meant as a Will, b) be written, and c) be signed using 2 witnesses. A Will not on paper like "Video Will", "Audio Will", or Will on a computer usually is invalid. Some states let ship crew, military, and people in emergencies do Oral Will told to someone but this should not be relied upon. Unlike some states Illinois does not let 2 witnesses be skipped if a person handwrites their full Will. Illinois law may allow remote signing or use of video conferencing but this is rarely used.

WITNESSES MUST BE AT LEAST 18 AND USUALLY NOT GETTING WILL GIFTS

<u>A person to act as witness must be at least age 18</u>. It is not required but preferable a witness not be old or live far away. A person who is named in a Will gift <u>can</u> witness the Will. But Will gifts to a witness are limited to what they'd get under intestate law if there was no Will (the law says they get that "which he would be entitled were [Will] not established"). To avoid the problem many people try to use "disinterested" witnesses who are not named in Will gifts. Though not required most people also try to not use a witness named in Will as Executor or as Guardian. Often used as a Will witness is a friend, stranger, or family.

TESTATOR AND 2 WITNESSES SIGN A WILL WHEN ALL TOGETHER

To complete a Will a Testator signs and then 2 witnesses sign usually within a few minutes. Everyone should be in 1 room and see each person sign. Witnesses usually quietly read the 1 paragraph they sign. Testator need not initial Will pages. Witnesses and Testator showing each other an ID is not required but is common. Testator or witness need not use their full legal name if they dislike it and rarely used it.

TESTATOR NEED NOT SAY ANYTHING WHEN SIGNING

A Testator when signing a Will in Illinois need not say anything. As option some people choose to say a thing like, "My name is ____ and this is the Will I want and do voluntarily and want you 2 people to witness". Some Testators also chat with witnesses a few minutes to help show they know what they're doing.

KEEP SIGNED WILL IN SAFE PLACE IT CAN BE FOUND AFTER A DEATH

Once done people should keep Will so it can be found within days of a death, like in desk, drawer, safe, or less often a safe deposit box. It can be given to a person to hold. It may help to tell people where to find a Will and any needed code or keys. Though rarely done a Will can be filed early at Probate Court for safekeeping.

MOST WILLS SAY USE LESS COSTLY AND SHORTER "INFORMAL" PROBATE
To help most Wills authorize "informal probate" which is a legal option to reduce some costs and delays. Usually probate after a death is not too costly or slow, and often over 95% of value gets to wanted persons.

MOST WILLS SAY TO SKIP COSTLY BOND
Most Wills say no "bond" or "surety" is needed for Executor, Guardian, or similar. Most people do not want a bond since it is insurance against misconduct paid with estate money and they trust people they named.

MOST WILLS HAVE A "MISCELLANEOUS" PART WITH HELPFUL LANGUAGE
Most Wills have a "Miscellaneous" part with paragraphs of legal language to avoid some legal problems.

CANCELING OLD WILLS IS USUALLY NOT A PROBLEM
So a new Will is followed old Wills should be canceled ("revoked") but this is easy and rarely a problem. A new Will often says old Wills are revoked to cancel them, and all the Will forms in this book start with this. To revoke a Will a person can also write "void" or "canceled" or "X" on a Will, preferably with a witness to this. Usually crossing out just part of a Will has no effect, and revoking a Will doesn't bring back an earlier Will.

WILL NAMES AN EXECUTOR TO DO THINGS AFTER A DEATH

CAN NAME A PERSON AS "EXECUTOR" TO DO THINGS AFTER A DEATH
Most people in their Will name someone as "Executor" to do things after their death. The law gives an Executor legal power to do things, like transfer property and money to new owners, order banks and others to transfer things, handle creditors, and do probate. Often a Will is written to give Executor more powers. If a Will does not name an Executor a judge can pick someone but family may argue about this choice. Often named as Executor is a spouse, family, or a friend. A lawyer or bank can be Executor if they agree and get a big fee. Naming 2 people to both do the job is possible but rare due to risk of arguments and delay, and since any 1 person named should be trusted. A person named to be Executor can get Will gifts. Instead of Executor the term "Administrator" can be used for person handling things after a death if a judge picked them, and the term "Personal Representative" can be used to mean both Executor and Administrator.

EXECUTOR CAN BE PAID AND ESTATE PAYS FOR MOST NEEDED THINGS
Many states let Executor ask for pay for their work and usually this is fairly small and fair. But pay is often not asked for to avoid income tax to Executor and leave more for Will gifts. Money an Executor needs like for court fees, attorneys, insurance, repairs, mortgage payments, and similar comes from estate assets.

EXECUTOR IS PERSON AT LEAST 18 AND SECOND PERSON RARELY NEEDED
In Illinois a person to be Executor must be 18 or older, be a U.S. legal resident, usually have no felony criminal record, and not be so disabled they can't do a good job. But being local can make the job easier. A judge can remove a person doing a bad job as Executor. Some people name a 2nd person to serve if the 1st person is unavailable, but most skip doing this since it's rarely needed, if seen a new Will can be done, or if needed a judge can pick someone. If people want to name a 2nd person to be Executor just in case some words can be added to Will, like: "or if they are reasonably unable to serve I name _____ to serve".

CHAPTER 4
WILL GIFTS INCLUDING RESIDUE

MAIN USE OF WILL IS TO SAY GIFTS TO HAPPEN AFTER DEATH
People use a Will mostly to say what happens to their property and money after their death, usually by making various Will gifts. Verbal and even most written statements about this are not usually valid if outside a Will. A Will can control property acquired after it was signed. Note, after a death some families if all agree may informally hand out small items in ways a decedent mentioned they wanted, but this is not fully proper.

GIFTING IN WILL USING SIMPLE WORDS OFTEN IS BEST
Making gifts in a Will using simple words is often best, using words like "I give to" and "I gift to". This is legally fine and avoids confusing legal words like "bequest", "devise", and "legacy" which few people know.

PEOPLE ARE MOSTLY FREE TO GIFT THEIR THINGS AS WANTED
People are mostly free to give at death their money and property as they want, like give a child nothing, give all to a charity, or give all to a friend. But family may have some rights which this book covers later.

IN WILL CAN DO "SPECIFIC GIFTS" TO GIFT PARTICULAR PROPERTY
Most Wills have "specific gifts" to gift <u>particular things</u>. These can be anything, like "I give boat to Ed Hu" and "I give UBank account #84553873 to Sue Wu". If a gift is not clear the law assumes all of a kind of thing is given, like "I give jewelry to Ann Po" means <u>all</u> jewelry. But gifting specific property can have risks like value of an item can change, or a Will gift may fail to occur later if property is no longer owned.

IN WILL CAN DO "GENERAL GIFTS" LIKE OF MONEY
Wills can do "general gifts" where what is gifted is not particular property but can be flexibly chosen, like "I give 1 of my 3 cars to Ed Po" which lets an Executor pick which car. The usual general gift is money, like "I give $5 to Ed Vu". Money gifts are easy to write, let equal gifts be made, and are safer since specific items might not be owned at death. To carry out money gifts an Executor uses accounts or sells some property.

"RESIDUE CLAUSE" IS CATCH-ALL THAT HELPFULLY GIFTS ANYTHING LEFT
Most Wills by their end have a Residue Clause to gift property or money not gifted or used in Will or other way, sometimes called a "catch-all" or "left-over" clause. <u>The Residue Clause is covered later in this Chapter</u>.

PROPERTY OR MONEY IN A "JOINT GIFT" GOES TO MULTIPLE PEOPLE
The same property or money in a "joint gift" can go to multiple people to each get a part interest, like "I give boat and all hats to Ann Wu and Sue Han" means each person owns 50% of every item. People later can split things by agreement or as Executor suggests, or Executor can sell items and split the money. If a person in a joint gift has died their part of things usually is left to transfer under a Residue Clause.

GIFT BENEFICIARIES CAN GET PERCENTAGE RATHER THAN EQUAL SHARE
If a Will gift goes to multiple people the law assumes equal shares, but if wanted <u>percentages can be put to make unequal gifts</u>, like "I give boat 90% to Ed Wu and 10% to Joe Hud".

OPTIONS EXIST TO HANDLE RARE CASE PERSON IN A WILL GIFT DIES

PERSON IN WILL GIFT USUALLY MUST SURVIVE OR GIFT DOES NOT OCCUR
Though rarely an issue, many Wills like this book's Will forms say a person named in a Will gift must survive (live past) the Testator or the gift will not later occur unless gift language specifically says different. If survival isn't required like this then what occurs can be unclear (for many reasons like certain state laws). Most people if they see a person in a gift has died just re-do a Will or trust a Residue Clause to handle it.

SOME PEOPLE ADD "ALTERNATE BENEFICIARY" MAYBE FOR SPECIAL ITEMS
Some people to handle if a person named in a Will gift dies maybe put for special items an alternate beneficiary, like for example: "I give oak table to Ed Wu but if they don't survive me to Ben Fox".

IF PERSON IN WILL GIFT DIES IT CAN GO TO "LINEAL DESCENDANTS"
A Will gift can say it goes to a person but if they don't survive the Testator then say the gift goes to the person's "lineal descendants". Descendants are a person's children and grandchildren. Also, the term "per stirpes" is often used to say to give to each family branch equally. An example shows how this works:

A Will may say: "All clothes to Sue Wu but if they don't survive to their lineal descendants per stirpes", and this means if Sue Wu has died and her son Ken Wu is living and her other son Ben Wu has died but left 2 children then, legally, by law Ken Wu himself gets 50% and Ben Wu's 2 children each get 25%.

HELPFUL LAWS OFTEN REQUIRE PERSON SURVIVE 120 HOURS TO GET GIFT
Laws in most states say a person dying within 120 hours of someone is seen as having died earlier, so often a Will gift to them is ignored. This avoids legal problems like need to know exact time of death and, also, having an item go through many probate legal cases over years.

CAN LEAVE SOME WILL GIFT LINES BLANK OR WRITE THINGS LIKE "SKIPPED"
A person writing a Will can choose to not use some gifts lines in a Will legal form, like by just leaving them blank, writing things like "SKIPPED" or "NONE" in them, or using a computer to delete some gift lines. Judges and others usually do not care about neatness or empty spaces in Wills.

"GIFT LISTS" ARE NOT LEGAL BUT SOME FAMILY DO FOLLOW THEM
Unlike many states Illinois law does not say a "List" or "Memo" outside the Will can add more gifts to be done after a person's death, and legally such writings should be ignored. Note, some families if no one objects do try to do transfers a person wrote on a note, wrote on stickers on items, or just mentioned.

CONDITIONS ON WILL GIFTS ARE RARE DUE TO POSSIBLE PROBLEMS
Putting conditions on a gift, like "I give Ann Poe $90 if she graduates college", can cause problems like years of delay, risk of lawsuits, and big attorneys fees, and due to this conditions are rarely put on Will gifts.

LATER DIVORCE OR MURDER CANCELS WILL GIFTS TO A PERSON
Illinois law says a person divorcing or murdering Testator usually cancels all Will gifts to the person.

RESIDUE CLAUSE GIFTING ALL LEFT IS MAIN WAY USED TO GIFT THINGS

THE "RESIDUE CLAUSE" IS CATCH-ALL THAT HELPS GIFT ANYTHING LEFT

Most Wills by their end have a Residue Clause to gift any property or money not gifted earlier in a Will or used in other ways. Things transferred this way is called the "Residue". Many people gift most their money and property this way by intentionally not mentioning in a Will most things so the Residue Clause handles it. This avoids need to describe things and has less legal risk. After applying a Residue Clause if anything is somehow left then by law a decedent's closest heirs-at-law get things (this is their closest family).

USUAL RESIDUE CLAUSE HAS 2 PARTS

A short 2 part Residue Clause is usual and is used in this book's Will forms, and it has:

1) 1st space to name 1 or more persons to get things if they survive Testator (many name a spouse or closest family here), and if several people are named but only some survive then survivors split things, and

2) 2nd space to name persons to get things if all in the 1st space don't survive (many people name next close family or friends in this space), and if a person in 2nd space has died their descendants get their share.

EXAMPLE OF 2 PART RESIDUE CLAUSE:

"RESIDUE CLAUSE: I give money and property not already gifted in earlier parts of this Will:
a) to __my husband John Paul Doe__ who survive me with persons just named who survive me taking the share of non-survivors, then
b) to __Sam Doe my son, Beth Wu my daughter, and Greta Fisher my friend__ and if any of those just named do not survive me their part goes to their lineal descendants per stirpes.

In this example if John Paul Doe has survived then he gets all things, but if John Paul Doe hasn't survived and also Sam Doe hasn't survived and he left 2 daughters then those 2 daughters split the 1/3 share of Sam Doe so get 1/6 each and other 2 persons in second part Beth Wu and Greta Fisher get 1/3 each.

PEOPLE CAN PUT SAME THING IN PARTS, OR SKIP PART, OR PUT PERCENTAGE

Some people put the same 1 person in both parts of a Residue Clause, to fully ensure that 1 person or if they later die their descendants will get things. Or a person with no spouse may skip the Residue Clause 1st part and in the 2nd part put their children (including any who died who had a child), so all branches of a family get an equal share. Many people use percentages in a Residue Clause to get the split wanted among people.

SOME PEOPLE CHANGE A RESIDUE CLAUSE TO HAVE 1 PART

Some people change a Residue Clause to have just 1 part since this can gift more equally and be easier to understand. *See example in Appendix.* For example a Residue Clause can be made to say:

"The rest, residue, and remainder of my estate, and anything else, I give to _____ who survive me and if any of those just named do not survive me their part goes to their lineal descendants per stirpes."

MUST SUFFICIENTLY DESCRIBE NAMES AND PROPERTY IN WILL GIFTS

WILL GIFT IS FINE IF PEOPLE CAN TELL WHAT TESTATOR LIKELY MEANT

The basic legal rule is a Will gift is sufficiently detailed if people who knew Testator can inform Executor or a judge what Testator meant more likely than not, and certainty is not needed to carry out a Will gift.

PUTTING NAMES OF PEOPLE OR GROUPS IN WILL GIFTS IS FAIRLY EASY

Names in Wills are fairly easy. It is assumed people gift to people they know so it's OK to use common names unless 2 friends or family have same name. Details can be added if names may not be recognized or to be friendly, like "I give $5 to waitress in town Ann Ax" and "I give $5 to my loyal funny friend Ed Grant". If people used a nickname "also known as" or "a/k/a" may help, like "I give $5 to Ed Wu a/k/a Old Fishy". Gifts can go to non-persons like a government, charity, or group if they're a real organization. Examples are: "I give $5 to The Salvation Army, "I give $5 to Joliet City Library", "I give $50 to Ivy School, Hilo, Hawaii", and "I give all clothes to Bethel Church in Elgin, IL". People often phone to ask for the full name of a charity.

DESCRIPTIONS OF ITEMS IN WILL GIFTS IS FAIRLY EASY

Describing items in Wills is fairly easy since people rarely own similar items that would cause confusion. So likely fine is "I give boat to Ed Wu" and "I give big bed to Don Ho". It's OK to gift by list or category, like "I give cow, van, and ax to Mark Smith" and "I give clothes to Ed Hill". Financial assets can use plain words, like "stocks" or "savings accounts at CitiBank", but details can help, like "UBank account ending in #2511". But judges may ignore gifts if it seems items were placed to affect gifting and not "independently significant" reason. So, "I give Ed Po items in desk" a judge may not follow, but "I give Ed Po boats at cabin" likely is OK.

DESCRIBING REAL PROPERTY IS HARD SO MANY USE RESIDUE OR TITLE

To give real property (real estate) in a Will using a "legal description" is legally best but is hard to do well. This can be paragraphs long, for example like: "Lot 3, Block 21 of Mann's Subdivision, Map Book 3, page 17, Records of Cook County, IL", or "Commence at NE Corner of the East ½ of West ½ of NE ¼ of SW ¼ of Section 17, T 1 North, R 12 West and then run S 100 ft, then run W 100 ft, and then go to point of beginning".

It is legally less safe but common to gift real property with plain words, like house by "I give 21 Ivy Rd., Bern, IL to Leo Hunt", or land like "I give all real property in Pine County, IL to Sue Ann Hu". A street address and legal description are often both used. Will gifts using a location give all real property and fixtures there.

But the legally safest way to gift real property is 1) do nothing specific so it's covered by Will Residue Clause which covers things not specifically gifted other ways, or 2) have broker or lawyer add names to the land title.

CHAPTER 5
DEBT, MARRIAGE, AND YOUNG CHILD ISSUES

DEBT, MARRIAGE, AND YOUNG CHILD CAN CAUSE ISSUES
This Chapter deals with debt, marriage, and young child. People may want to do research on their state.

DEBT ISSUES

PAYING DECEDENT'S DEBTS MAY USE UP RESOURCES AND REDUCE GIFTS
Creditors owed by decedent can ask a judge to be paid from decedent's money and property before Will gifts are carried out. But if decedent had under $50,000 of money and things plus house any creditors often do not bother, for reasons explained below. Resources to pay debts come from (in order) the Will Residue, Will general gifts like money, Will specific gifts, and then other transfers. Some debts like for probate costs, attorneys, funeral, and medical debts have priority to be paid earlier. Family usually are not personally liable for decedent's debts unless they guaranteed or co-signed them, but a spouse may owe health care costs. People should consider how paying debts may use up estate resources leaving less to carry out Will gifts.

BEFORE DEBTS ARE PAID MAY COME SOME FAMILY RIGHTS
Most states say spouse or minor children have "family rights" they can claim before most debts are paid, which helps family get something even if decedent had debts. Many states give family a "year allowance" and rights to "exempt property" and other rights. Illinois is a bit different but does let any spouse claim $20,000 and each minor child $10,000 of decedent's things or more if it is needed in the year after a death. Since family rights may use money and property if they are claimed often a person by Will and other ways gives mostly to family (like over 50% and the home) so they don't bother to use these family rights.

"HOMESTEAD EXEMPTION" PROTECTS HOME FOR FAMILY FROM DEBTS
"Homestead" laws in most states say decedent's creditors usually can't involve decedent's home if Decedent has a spouse or minor children. Often these laws also say spouse or minor children get ownership of decedent's house (or use for their life in some states) if decedent owned it and despite what a Will says. Illinois law is a bit different and just says decedent's house going to a spouse must have over $30,000 equity before creditors can involve it in collection efforts. This amount is $15,000 if a house goes to children. Importantly, Illinois lets married couples hold house jointly as "tenants by the entirety" so it passes to the surviving spouse and then isn't usually affected at all by debts only owed by the deceased spouse. Due to all this most people give any spouse or any minor children the house by Will or by naming them on the title. Of course a valid mortgage, home equity loan, mechanics lien, or similar if not paid usually can be foreclosed.

USUALLY SECURED DEBTS LIKE MORTGAGE OR VEHICLE LIEN ARE NOT PAID
Usually laws say any secured debts like house mortgage or car lien are not paid off after a death but remain, even if a Will says generally to pay debts. This book's Will forms say this. This avoids using up estate resources on paying off secured debts so more is left to carry out other Will gifts. Of course people who get a house or car with a secured debt usually must make monthly loan payments to keep the property. If a Testator wants to help pay off secured debts they can a) in a Will also give a person enough cash to pay them off, or b) add order to pay in Will (like "I order mortgage on the cabin paid off").

MARRIAGE ISSUES

MOST STATES USE "SEPARATE PROPERTY LAW" FOR SPOUSES

Most states including Illinois use "Separate Property" law saying married people mostly own money, property, and income separately. Due to this a spouse is mostly free to sell during life their things, or gift in their Will their things with some small exceptions. But joint ownership by 2 spouses can arise by agreement, paying half a purchase price, and also many spouses do paperwork to own a house jointly.

"COMMUNITY PROPERTY" LAW APPLIES IN OTHER STATES FOR SPOUSES

There are 9 states mostly in West and South U.S.A. that use "Community Property" law for spouses, such as California, Texas, Washington, and Wisconsin. This law says if a married person lives in these states then most property or money gotten is usually owned 50/50 by spouses as "Community Property" if it relates to labor, effort, or time while married. Community Property also includes items bought or just improved with other Community Property, or anything just mixed in with any Community Property. Most people avoid these issues unless moving to or from these states.

"JOINT WILL" SIGNED BY BOTH SPOUSES IS NOT RECOMMENDED

Some couples sign 1 "Joint Will" written by a lawyer saying spouses gives all to the other if they die first, then saying last living spouse gives to all children equally, and usually it says a spouse may not change this. Joint Wills are not recommended and banned in some states and most people dislike how restrictive it is.

SPOUSE CAN SEEK "ELECTIVE SHARE" IF UNHAPPY WITH WHAT THEY GET

Most states using Separate Property law (like Illinois) for fairness give spouse if unhappy with what a Will gifts them a right to choose (elect) an "Elective Share" of their spouse's property and money instead. Illinois keeps it simple and sets the Elective Share as 1/2 normally and at 1/3 if a decedent also left descendants like children. To avoid tricks an Elective Share by law can cover more, like items a spouse gave away recently or controls but doesn't own. If an Elective Share is used to claim 1/2 or 1/3 then any Will gifts to the electing spouse are not carried out, but Will gifts to other people are carried out if possible. Because of all this often a married person gifts by Will and other ways mostly to a spouse (often 50% and family house) to avoid them being upset and using the Elective Share law to get more money and property.

YOUNG CHILD ISSUES

CAN NAME "GUARDIAN OF THE PERSON" TO CARE FOR CHILD

If a parent dies with a minor child under 18 the other natural or adopted parent (but not step-parent) automatically takes over daily care (and related issues like school, discipline, and health care) unless the other parent is unavailable or proven unfit in court which is rare. But just in case it is needed a Will can name someone as "Guardian of the Person" to do this daily care and control related issues for a child.

MOST NAME HEALTHY RELATIVE OR FRIEND AS GUARDIAN OF THE PERSON

Since naming the other parent is pointless (they take over if not unavailable or proven unfit) most parents in a Will name as Guardian of the Person a healthy adult friend or relative just in case needed. If needed and no Will names a person a judge can pick someone (often close family) after a court hearing. The preference of last living parent has more weight. Naming 2 persons to both do this is rare since they may argue and any 1 person named should be trusted, but some people do name a stable married couple.

CAN NAME "GUARDIAN OF THE ESTATE" TO MANAGE ASSETS OF CHILD

In a Will someone can be named as "Guardian of the Estate" to help in the very rare cases a young child gets or owns any property or money. This Guardian manages the money and property owned by a child and decides what school, health care, and other living costs to pay for till usually at 18 anything left goes to the child. People giving a child a home or necessities can ask to be paid from the child's money and property. Judges often hold a yearly hearing reviewing what a Guardian of the Estate has paid for.

MOST NAME OTHER PARENT AS GUARDIAN OF THE ESTATE

Most people in a Will name the other parent as Guardian of the Estate since they usually know what spending is needed, care about child, and may argue with anyone else. Or a parent can name someone else to be Guardian of the Estate if they want (like a relative or a friend), maybe because the other parent is bad with money or unreliable. Naming 2 persons to both do this job is rare since they may argue and any 1 person named should be trusted, but some people name a stable married couple. Later if the named person is not available (including due to death though this is very rare) a judge can pick someone else.

GUARDIANS MUST BE ADULT, RESIDENT OF U.S., AND NOT FELON

Under Illinois law to be any kind of Guardian a person must at least 18, legal resident of the country, usually have no felony criminal conviction, and not be too disabled to do the job. Most people don't worry about a Guardian not being available since this is rare and a judge can name someone, but people who want can modify a Will to name a 2nd person, like: "or if they are unable to serve I nominate _____ to serve". Some people to keep things simple name the same 1 person to be both kinds of Guardian and be Executor.

PICKING GUARDIANS RARELY MATTERS DESPITE PARENTS WORRYING

A young child having parents die is rare, so parents naming people like a Guardian to help rarely matters. A study of 311,900 people found 72,240 were under 18 and of these 2014 had lost 1 parent (2.78%) and just 97 both parents (just 0.13%), so losing parents is very rare. *Census Life Factors Mortality Study #288*. About half of these children shared common parents so odds for each family are even less.

CHAPTER 6
BASIC IDEAS ABOUT HEALTH CARE FORMS

SOME BASIC IDEAS HELP UNDERSTANDING OF HEALTH CARE LEGAL FORMS

Some ideas help people understand health care forms.

■ By law people controls their own health care by telling medical personnel what they want <u>unless they are "incapacitated"</u> by insufficient ability to a) <u>communicate</u> verbally or by notes, b) be <u>rational</u>, or c) be <u>conscious</u>. Most people keep control of their own care till death or till no big treatment options remain, but some people worry they may be incapacitated a long time so want to do health care forms.

■ Legal documents that help control health care are usually called "Advanced Directives".

■ If an adult 18 or older becomes incapacitated <u>the adult's closest family like spouse or adult child usually can make emergency decisions</u>. But later they usually must then rush to a judge to get further power if no legal document gives them more power over health care.

■ In legal documents a <u>person can be named to have control of health care</u> if needed. This person is often called the "Health Care Agent", "Health Care Attorney-in-Fact", "Health Care Advocate", or a similar name.

■ In legal documents people can <u>write medical instructions that doctors, family, and other people must obey</u>.

■ Parents even without legal documents mostly have <u>full</u> power over health care of <u>children under age 18</u>, and the only exception is teens have some freedom to pick their own family planning or gender related care.

■ Some <u>married people</u> do documents to give a spouse power over medical care if they are incapacitated. Some adults especially <u>to age 25</u> do documents to give this power to parents. The young are less often sick.

■ Pain relief like pain drugs or comfort care is still given even if documents say to stop or limit other care.

■ <u>Most people only do 1 legal document</u> about health care that often names someone to control health care if needed and has a spot for basic instructions (this is sometimes called a "Health Care Power of Attorney").

■ For the rare times stopping health care seems more likely to matter (like due to extreme illness or old age):

-- most people do nothing special and trust family or Health Care Agent to wisely decide when to stop care (they can weigh many factors like pain, cost, likely difficulty of treatment, beliefs, and chances of recovery);

-- a few people do a serious document to say to stop most health care if <u>later</u> doctors think an incapacitated person has very bad health and more medical care likely won't help (sometimes this is called a "Living Will";

-- a few people do a serious document to say <u>starting immediately</u> to not give most medical care (often this is called a "Do-Not-Resuscitate" if about resuscitation, or called a "Physician's Order" if about many treatments).

CHAPTER 7
FORM 1: WILL (STANDARD)

FORM 1 IS A STANDARD WILL THAT IS FLEXIBLE WITH NO GUARDIANS

Form 1 is a standard Will that is flexible and is the Will form most people use. It has no part about guardians or similar so is usually for person with no child under age 18. The term "Last Will And Testament" is used to start a Will since in the past a "Testament" was a legal document often done with a Will.

WILL IN FORM 1 HAS BASIC LAYOUT WITH SEVERAL PARTS

The Will at its start has place for person doing the Will (Testator) to write their name and county.

The 1st paragraph, "Gifts", has many spaces to make either specific gifts of particular property or general gifts like of money. People can delete, copy and paste to add more, or leave blank these gift lines.

The 2nd paragraph, "Residue", has a Residue Clause to gift property and money left after other Will parts to those persons named here.

The 3rd paragraph, "Administration", has space to name an "Executor" to handle legal and other matters after death.

The 4th paragraph, "Miscellaneous", has sentences of legal language to help avoid certain legal issues.

Last is a paragraph for person doing Will to date and sign, and 2 witnesses to sign and give addresses.

USUAL RESIDUE CLAUSE HAS 2 PLACES TO NAME PERSONS TO GET THINGS

In "Residue Clause" of Will anything left after other Will parts is gifted to persons who are named here. Many people use a Residue Clause to gift most things. In the Residue Clause in this book's Will there is:

1) a 1st space to name 1 or more persons to get the residue, and if any named here have not survived and died before the Will maker then any other persons named here take their share,

2) a 2nd space to name people to get things if all in 1st space died before Will maker (these are "fallbacks") and if any people named here didn't survive their shares go to "lineal descendants" like their children.

Most people name in 1st space a spouse or closest family or closest friends, and in 2nd space next closest family or friends. This may seem complicated but usually those in 1st area of Residue Clause get things.

TESTATOR SIGNS WILL AND THEN 2 WITNESSES SIGN

A Will after being filled out by computer or by hand in pen or pencil (except bits intentionally left blank) then should be signed by person doing Will ("Testator") before 2 witnesses at least age 18 who sign too. It is usually best to use witnesses not getting gifts in Will and not named Executor or Guardian in the Will. For signing use pen or marker with permanent ink not pencil, and Testator and 2 witnesses should be in same room and see each other sign. Witnesses only read the 1 paragraph they sign and not the full Will. It is optional but some Testators say to witnesses a thing like "This is my Will" and may hold Will up, and some also chat a few minutes with witnesses to show they are of sound mind and not being forced.

LAST WILL AND TESTAMENT

I, _____, of _____ County, Illinois, do revoke all prior Wills, Testaments, and Codicils, and do make, publish, and declare this to be my Will. When doing this I am of sound mind and under no duress or undue influence.

1. GIFTS. I give these gifts in this Will, but to get a gift in this section the recipient must survive me except as otherwise stated below.

I give _____ to _____.

I give _____ to _____.

I give _____ to _____.

I give _____ to _____.

I give _____ to _____.

I give _____ to _____.

I give _____ to _____.

I give _____ to _____.

I give _____ to _____.

I give _____ to _____.

I give _____ to _____.

I give _____ to _____.

2. RESIDUE. I give the rest and residue and remainder of my estate, my money and property of any kind and nature, and anything I have an interest in so long as it was not transferred by other Will provisions (all of which is called the "residue"), as follows:

a) to _____ who survive me with persons just named who survive me taking the share of non-survivors, then

b) to _____ and if any of those just named do not survive me their part goes to their lineal descendants per stirpes.

3. ADMINISTRATION. I name and appoint _____
as Executor including for me, my Will, and my estate.

4. MISCELLANEOUS. The following applies to this Will and generally.

Priority of Will gifts of the same type is based on the order they are written.

The words "give" and "gift" also means a devise, bequest, grant, legacy, or similar.

If gift or gift section mentions survival, survive, or surviving then survival is an absolute condition and anti-lapse laws or similar have no effect.

In this document no unfilled part is a mistake and residue spaces may be left blank.

Any failure to make gifts to family including children is intentional and not a mistake.

No gift or transfer made during life reduces or offsets a Will gift unless during my life I expressly called it a "loan" or "advancement".

Use of particular gender shall include other genders, reference to singular or plural shall be interchangeable, and "they" may be singular or plural.

If context permits the terms Executor, Personal Representative, and Administrator shall be seen as interchangeable as if all were written, and if context permits Guardian of the Estate is interchangeable with Guardian of the Property and with Conservator.

Any person named or acting as Executor may anytime pay or settle claims or debts they in their sole discretion find proper or helpful to pay, but I specifically say any secured debts including mortgages or liens on real property or vehicles should not be paid off unless parts of this Will specify it.

I give any person named or acting as Executor the fullest power and discretion allowed by state law, and I grant them all powers that may be conferred on Executors by state law.

Any person named or acting as Executor shall not be required to render and file annual accountings with respect to property or money including in relation to my Will or estate.

I authorize informal probate of my estate and Will and also administrative probate if any Executor chooses, and any Executor may act independently in all ways without supervision including from any court or judge.

I give any person named or acting as Executor authority to lease, sell, mortgage, convey, or retain property of mine in such manner and time they deem helpful or proper.

The residue includes lapsed or failed gifts, insurance paid to estate, inheritances owed me, and property I had a power of appointment or testamentary disposition over.

If in any place a Guardian of the Estate, Conservator, Administrator, Guardian of the Property, or any other fiduciary is needed for a child of mine or their estate or property, or for any other person, then I appoint for that the person named Executor above.

Any Executor, Personal Representative, Guardian, Administrator, Conservator, or fiduciary shall qualify and serve without bond, surety, security, or similar, including

despite their place of residence or lack of relationship to any state or country.

I name as Custodian under the Illinois Uniform Transfers to Minors Act or a similar law anywhere the person named in this Will as Guardian of the Estate or if they are unable to serve the person named Executor. An Executor using their sole discretion has power to at any time transfer money or property of a child or mine or any minor to this Custodian to serve under the Act until the minor is 18, and all without bond or any court action.

TESTATOR

IN WITNESS WHEREOF, I, _____, have signed, published, and declared this document as my Will, this _____ day of _____, 20____.

_____
Testator signature

WITNESSES

We, the persons who sign below as witnesses to this Will, certify and attest that in presence of all witnesses on the date shown on this Will

that _____ as Testator signed the Will and acknowledged it to be Testator's Will, and

that we witnesses at Testator's request and in presence of all other witnesses and Testator have signed our names as witnesses to the Will and attested the Will, and

that all the witnesses believed Testator to be of sound mind and memory at the time of signing the Will.

_____ _____
Witness signature Witness address

_____ _____
Witness signature Witness address

CHAPTER 8
FORM 2: WILL (GUARDIANS)

FORM 2 IS BASIC WILL WITH GUARDIANS CLAUSE FOR THOSE NEEDING THIS

Form 2 is a Will with Guardians clause for a parent or similar person who has any child under age 18. The term "Last Will And Testament" is used since a Testament was a legal document often done with a Will.

WILL IN FORM 2 HAS BASIC LAYOUT WITH SEVERAL PARTS

The Will at its start has place for person doing the Will (Testator) to write their name and county.

The 1st paragraph, "Gifts", has many spaces to make either specific gifts of particular property or general gifts like of money. People can delete, copy and paste to add more, or leave blank these gift lines.

The 2nd paragraph, "Residue", has a Residue Clause to gift property and money left after other Will parts to those persons named here.

The 3rd paragraph, "Administration", has space to name an "Executor" to handle legal and other matters after death.

<u>The 4th paragraph, "Guardians", lets "Guardian of the Person" be named to care for child or similar person, and also "Guardian of the Estate" be named to manage such persons property and money.</u>

The 5th paragraph, "Miscellaneous", has sentences of legal language to help avoid certain legal issues.

Last is a paragraph for person doing Will to date and sign, and 2 witnesses to sign and give addresses.

USUAL RESIDUE CLAUSE HAS 2 PLACES TO NAME PERSONS TO GET THINGS

In "Residue Clause" of Will anything left after other Will parts is gifted to persons who are named here. Many people use a Residue Clause to gift most things. In the Residue Clause in this book's Will there is:

1) a 1st space to name 1 or more persons to get the residue, and if any named here have not survived and died before the Will maker then any other persons named here take their share,

2) a 2nd space to name people to get things if all in 1st space died before Will maker (these are "fallbacks") and if any people named here didn't survive their shares go to "lineal descendants" like their children.

Most people name in 1st space a spouse or closest family or closest friends, and in 2nd space next closest family or friends. This may seem complicated but usually those in 1st area of Residue Clause get things.

TESTATOR SIGNS WILL AND THEN 2 WITNESSES SIGN

A Will after being filled out by computer or by hand in pen or pencil (except bits intentionally left blank) then should be signed by person doing Will ("Testator") before 2 witnesses at least age 18 who sign too. It is usually best to use witnesses not getting gifts in Will and not named Executor or Guardian in the Will. For signing use pen or marker with permanent ink not pencil, and Testator and 2 witnesses should be in same room and see each other sign. Witnesses only read the 1 paragraph they sign and not the full Will. It is optional but some Testators say to witnesses a thing like "This is my Will" and may hold Will up, and some also chat a few minutes with witnesses to show they are of sound mind and not being forced.

LAST WILL AND TESTAMENT

I, _____, of _____ County, Illinois, do revoke all prior Wills, Testaments, and Codicils, and do make, publish, and declare this to be my Will. When doing this I am of sound mind and under no duress or undue influence.

1. GIFTS. I give these gifts in this Will, but to get a gift in this section the recipient must survive me except as otherwise stated below.

I give _____ to _____.

I give _____ to _____.

I give _____ to _____.

I give _____ to _____.

I give _____ to _____.

I give _____ to _____.

I give _____ to _____.

I give _____ to _____.

I give _____ to _____.

I give _____ to _____.

I give _____ to _____.

I give _____ to _____.

2. RESIDUE. I give the rest and residue and remainder of my estate, my money and property of any kind and nature, and anything I have an interest in so long as it was not transferred by other Will provisions (all of which is called the "residue"), as follows:

a) to _____ who survive me with persons just named who survive me taking the share of non-survivors, then

b) to _____ and if any of those just named do not survive me their part goes to their lineal descendants per stirpes.

3. ADMINISTRATION. I name and appoint _____
as Executor including for me, my Will, and my estate.

4. GUARDIANS. I name and nominate _____ as Guardian of the Person of any minor child of mine or any other person without full legal capacity. I also name and nominate _____ as Guardian of the Estate of any minor child of mine or other person without full legal capacity, and this person I name should be guardian for their money, property, and estate.

5. MISCELLANEOUS. The following applies to this Will and generally.

Priority of Will gifts of the same type is based on the order they are written.

The words "give" and "gift" also means a devise, bequest, grant, legacy, or similar.

If gift or gift section mentions survival, survive, or surviving then survival is an absolute condition and anti-lapse laws or similar have no effect.

In this document no unfilled part is a mistake and residue spaces may be left blank.

Any failure to make gifts to family including children is intentional and not a mistake.

No gift or transfer made during life reduces or offsets a Will gift unless during my life I expressly called it a "loan" or "advancement".

Use of particular gender shall include other genders, reference to singular or plural shall be interchangeable, and "they" may be singular or plural.

If context permits the terms Executor, Personal Representative, and Administrator shall be seen as interchangeable as if all were written, and if context permits Guardian of the Estate is interchangeable with Guardian of the Property and with Conservator.

Any person named or acting as Executor may anytime pay or settle claims or debts they in their sole discretion find proper or helpful to pay, but I specifically say any secured debts including mortgages or liens on real property or vehicles should not be paid off unless parts of this Will specify it.

I give any person named or acting as Executor the fullest power and discretion allowed by state law, and I grant them all powers that may be conferred on Executors by state law.

Any person named or acting as Executor shall not be required to render and file annual accountings with respect to property or money including in relation to my Will or estate.

I authorize informal probate of my estate and Will and also administrative probate if any Executor chooses, and any Executor may act independently in all ways without supervision including from any court or judge.

I give any person named or acting as Executor authority to lease, sell, mortgage, convey, or retain property of mine in such manner and time they deem helpful or proper.

The residue includes lapsed or failed gifts, insurance paid to estate, inheritances owed me, and property I had a power of appointment or testamentary disposition over.

If in any place a Guardian of the Estate, Conservator, Administrator, Guardian of the Property, or any other fiduciary is needed for a child of mine or their estate or property, or for any other person, then I appoint for that the person named Executor above.

Any Executor, Personal Representative, Guardian, Administrator, Conservator, or fiduciary shall qualify and serve without bond, surety, security, or similar, including despite their place of residence or lack of relationship to any state or country.

I name as Custodian under the Illinois Uniform Transfers to Minors Act or a similar law anywhere the person named in this Will as Guardian of the Estate or if they are unable to serve the person named Executor. An Executor using their sole discretion has power to at any time transfer money or property of a child or mine or any minor to this Custodian to serve under the Act until the minor is 18, and all without bond or any court action.

TESTATOR

IN WITNESS WHEREOF, I, _____, have signed, published, and declared this document as my Will, this _____ day of _____, 20____.

_____
Testator signature

WITNESSES

We, the persons who sign below as witnesses to this Will, certify and attest that in presence of all witnesses on the date shown on this Will

that _____ as Testator signed the Will and acknowledged it to be Testator's Will, and

that we witnesses at Testator's request and in presence of all other witnesses and Testator have signed our names as witnesses to the Will and attested the Will, and

that all the witnesses believed Testator to be of sound mind and memory at the time of signing the Will.

_____   _____
Witness signature   Witness address

_____   _____
Witness signature   Witness address

CHAPTER 9
FORM 3: SELF-PROVING AFFIDAVIT

FORM CAN BE DONE TO SUPPORT A WILL BUT IS OFTEN SKIPPED

The "Self-Proving Affidavit" form can be done with a Will to reduce later legal work. But as explained below this form is usually skipped in Illinois. If this form is done a person who is a notary must be used.

FORM CAN SAVE LATER WORK WHEN USING WILL

A Self-Proving Affidavit can later help "prove" a Will was properly signed. If this form is not done some work may be needed after a death to use a Will, and there is a bit more legal risk a Will is not followed later. But of people doing Wills in Illinois over half skip doing a Self-Proving Affidavit mostly due to the hassle of using a notary and since for legal reasons it isn't that necessary. Some lawyers to use a Self-Proving Affidavit to be extra careful. Some states have no Self-Proving Affidavit form at all.

IN ILLINOIS JUST SIGNATURES ON WILL OFTEN ENOUGH TO LATER USE WILL

Illinois law unlike most states says the signatures of the 2 witnesses on a Will is enough proof to use a Will after Testator's death, unless a family member or other person requests more proof which is very rare. In the rare cases more proof is requested this is usually not a problem and the people who are getting money and property using the Will are often happy to do it. Due to all this using a Self-Proving Affidavit is not seen as standard in Illinois and most people skip this form unless things are unusual.

FORM IS DONE BY TESTATOR AND 2 WITNESSES SIGNING BEFORE NOTARY

To do the form Testator and the 2 witnesses to the Will's signing must sign the Self-Proving Affidavit form in front of a notary who then notiarizes it. The Self-Proving Affidavit form is often done within minutes of when a Will is signed, but it also can be done anytime later (even many months) when Testator and 2 witnesses can arrange to all meet a notary. A Self-Proving Affidavit if often kept with the Will it supports.

SELF-PROVING AFFIDAVIT

STATE OF ILLINOIS   )
) ss.
COUNTY OF _____)

    We, the persons who sign below as witnesses, being first duly sworn, do hereby declare to the undersigned authority that
    while we were present as witnesses to a Will being signed _____ did sign in the presence of both of us that Will as the Testator of it,
    that this Testator signed that Will willingly as the Testator's free and voluntary act for the purposes set forth set forth in the document,
    that each of us witnesses in the presence of this Testator and in the presence of each other signed as a witness to that Will, and
    that to the best of our knowledge the Testator was at the time of signing of that Will of sound mind and memory and under no constraint or undue influence.

_____   _____
Witness signature   Witness address

_____   _____
Witness signature   Witness address

NOTARY OR OFFICER

    Signed and sworn to before me on this _____ day of _____, 20____, by _____ and _____, witnesses.

(Seal)   _____
                                Notary Public, State of Illinois

CHAPTER 10
FORM 4: STATUTORY SHORT FORM
POWER OF ATTORNEY FOR HEALTH CARE

FORM CAN NAME SOMEONE TO HELP CONTROL HEALTH CARE

This form lets a person name someone to make health care decisions and give some instructions. This form is a statutory form found in state law to use if wanted. At the start of the form is a few page "Notice" that explains things about the form. <u>Many people do this 1 form and skip other health care forms</u>.

CAN NAME "AGENT" TO MAKE HEALTH CARE DECISIONS IF NEEDED

The form lets a person doing the form (called the "Principal") name someone at least age 18 to be "Health Care Agent" to have power over health care if person doing the form is incapacitated so can't control their own health care (due to insufficient ability to communicate, be rational, or stay conscious). Often named as Agent is spouse, other family, or friend. Naming a family member as Agent in the form can avoid them the hassle of going to a judge to get more power in some situations. The form has a spot to name a "Successor" person to act if needed but most people skip this since it is rarely needed.

FORM HAS OPTIONS TO CHECK OR NOT AND SPOT FOR INSTRUCTIONS

The form has some options to check if a person wants about their Agent and health care. In the form instructions and limits the Agent must follow can be written. But many people skip writing instructions or limits since it is hard to not be a bit vague or unclear since health care is so complex, and this can cause legal problems or delays in treatment. Many people instead of writing anything just trust their Agent to do what was discussed with them or to make wise decisions.

PERSON SIGNS FORM WITH 1 WITNESS

The form is signed by person doing the form and 1 witness at least 18 (some people use 2 witnesses especially if they may be outside the state). The witness must a) not be named in form Agent or Successor (or married to these), b) not be employee, owner, or tied to hospital or any place giving care, and c) not be a relative of the person doing the form (not parent, child, sister or brother, or cousin - or married to these). Using a video-conference for "electronic signing" is now allowed in Illinois but this is almost never done. The form should be shown to all doctors and places that may be used to add it to medical files to follow. To cancel the form a person should tell Agent and probably tell people shown form to no longer follow it.

STATUTORY SHORT FORM POWER OF ATTORNEY FOR HEALTH CARE

NOTICE TO THE INDIVIDUAL SIGNING THE POWER OF ATTORNEY FOR HEALTH CARE

No one can predict when a serious illness or accident might occur. When it does, you may need someone else to speak or make health care decisions for you. If you plan now, you can increase the chances that the medical treatment you get will be the treatment you want.

In Illinois, you can choose someone to be your "health care agent". Your agent is the person you trust to make health care decisions for you if you are unable or do not want to make them yourself. These decisions should be based on your personal values and wishes.

It is important to put your choice of agent in writing. The written form is often called an "advance directive". You may use this form or another form, as long as it meets the legal requirements of Illinois. There are many written and online resources to guide you and your loved ones in having a conversation about these issues. You may find it helpful to look at these resources while thinking about and discussing your advance directive.

WHAT ARE THE THINGS I WANT MY HEALTH CARE AGENT TO KNOW?

The selection of your agent should be considered carefully, as your agent will have the ultimate decision-making authority once this document goes into effect, in most instances after you are no longer able to make your own decisions. While the goal is for your agent to make decisions in keeping with your preferences and in the majority of circumstances that is what happens, please know that the law does allow your agent to make decisions to direct or refuse health care interventions or withdraw treatment. Your agent will need to think about conversations you have had, your personality, and how you handled important health care issues in the past. Therefore, it is important to talk with your agent and your family about such things as:

(i) What is most important to you in your life?
(ii) How important is it to you to avoid pain and suffering?
(iii) If you had to choose, is it more important to you to live as long as possible, or to avoid prolonged suffering or disability?
(iv) Would you rather be at home or in a hospital for the last days or weeks of your life?
(v) Do you have religious, spiritual, or cultural beliefs that you want your agent and others to consider?
(vi) Do you wish to make a significant contribution to medical science after your death through organ or whole body donation?
(vii) Do you have an existing advance directive, such as a living will, that contains your specific wishes about health care that is only delaying your death? If you have another advance directive, make sure to discuss with your agent the directive and the treatment decisions contained within that outline your preferences. Make sure that your agent agrees to honor the wishes expressed in your advance directive.

WHAT KIND OF DECISIONS CAN MY AGENT MAKE?

If there is ever a period of time when your physician determines that you cannot make your own health care decisions, or if you do not want to make your own decisions, some of the

decisions your agent could make are to:
  (i) talk with physicians and other health care providers about your condition.
  (ii) see medical records and approve who else can see them.
  (iii) give permission for medical tests, medicines, surgery, or other treatments.
  (iv) choose where you receive care and which physicians and others provide it.
  (v) decide to accept, withdraw, or decline treatments designed to keep you alive if you are near death or not likely to recover. You may choose to include guidelines and/or restrictions to your agent's authority.
  (vi) agree or decline to donate your organs or your whole body if you have not already made this decision yourself. This could include donation for transplant, research, and/or education. You should let your agent know whether you are registered as a donor in the First Person Consent registry maintained by the Illinois Secretary of State or whether you have agreed to donate your whole body for medical research and/or education.
  (vii) decide what to do with your remains after you die, if you have not already made plans.
  (viii) talk with your other loved ones to help come to a decision (but your designated agent will have the final say over your other loved ones).

Your agent is not automatically responsible for your health care expenses.

WHOM SHOULD I CHOOSE TO BE MY HEALTH CARE AGENT?

You can pick a family member, but you do not have to. Your agent will have the responsibility to make medical treatment decisions, even if other people close to you might urge a different decision. The selection of your agent should be done carefully, as he or she will have ultimate decision-making authority for your treatment decisions once you are no longer able to voice your preferences. Choose a family member, friend, or other person who:
  (i) is at least 18 years old;
  (ii) knows you well;
  (iii) you trust to do what is best for you and is willing to carry out your wishes, even if he or she may not agree with your wishes;
  (iv) would be comfortable talking with and questioning your physicians and other health care providers;
  (v) would not be too upset to carry out your wishes if you became very sick; and
  (vi) can be there for you when you need it and is willing to accept this important role.

WHAT IF MY AGENT IS NOT AVAILABLE OR IS UNWILLING TO MAKE DECISIONS FOR ME?

If the person who is your first choice is unable to carry out this role, then the second agent you chose will make the decisions; if your second agent is not available, then the third agent you chose will make the decisions. The second and third agents are called your successor agents and they function as back-up agents to your first choice agent and may act only one at a time and in the order you list them.

WHAT WILL HAPPEN IF I DO NOT CHOOSE A HEALTH CARE AGENT?

If you become unable to make your own health care decisions and have not named an agent in writing, your physician and other health care providers will ask a family member, friend, or guardian to make decisions for you. In Illinois, a law directs which of these individuals will be consulted. In that law, each of these individuals is called a "surrogate".

There are reasons why you may want to name an agent rather than rely on a surrogate:

(i) The person or people listed by this law may not be who you would want to make decisions for you.

(ii) Some family members or friends might not be able or willing to make decisions as you would want them to.

(iii) Family members and friends may disagree with one another about the best decisions.

(iv) Under some circumstances, a surrogate may not be able to make the same kinds of decisions that an agent can make.

WHAT IF THERE IS NO ONE AVAILABLE WHOM I TRUST TO BE MY AGENT?

In this situation, it is especially important to talk to your physician and other health care providers and create written guidance about what you want or do not want, in case you are ever critically ill and cannot express your own wishes. You can complete a living will. You can also write your wishes down and/or discuss them with your physician or other health care provider and ask him or her to write it down in your chart. You might also want to use written or online resources to guide you through this process.

WHAT DO I DO WITH THIS FORM ONCE I COMPLETE IT?

Follow these instructions after you have completed the form:

(i) Sign the form in front of a witness. See the form for a list of who can and cannot witness it.

(ii) Ask the witness to sign it, too.

(iii) There is no need to have the form notarized.

(iv) Give a copy to your agent and to each of your successor agents.

(v) Give another copy to your physician.

(vi) Take a copy with you when you go to the hospital.

(vii) Show it to your family and friends and others who care for you.

WHAT IF I CHANGE MY MIND?

You may change your mind at any time. If you do, tell someone who is at least 18 years old that you have changed your mind, and/or destroy your document and any copies. If you wish, fill out a new form and make sure everyone you gave the old form to has a copy of the new one, including, but not limited to, your agents and your physicians. If you are concerned you may revoke your power of attorney at a time when you may need it the most, you may initial the box at the end of the form to indicate that you would like a 30-day waiting period after you voice your intent to revoke your power of attorney. This means if your agent is making decisions for you during that time, your agent can continue to make decisions on your behalf. This election is purely optional, and you do not have to choose it. If you do not choose this option, you can change your mind and revoke the power of attorney at any time.

WHAT IF I DO NOT WANT TO USE THIS FORM?

In the event you do not want to use the Illinois statutory form provided here, any document you complete must be executed by you, designate an agent who is over 18 years of age and not prohibited from serving as your agent, and state the agent's powers, but it need not be witnessed or conform in any other respect to the statutory health care power.

If you have questions about the use of any form, you may want to consult your physician, other health care provider, and/or an attorney.

MY POWER OF ATTORNEY FOR HEALTH CARE

THIS POWER OF ATTORNEY REVOKES ALL PREVIOUS POWERS OF ATTORNEY FOR HEALTH CARE. (You must sign this form and a witness must also sign it before it is valid)

My name (Print your full name): _____

My address: _____

I WANT THE FOLLOWING PERSON TO BE MY HEALTH CARE AGENT

(an agent is your personal representative under state and federal law):

(Agent name) _____ (Agent phone number) _____

(Agent address) _____

(Please check box if applicable) [ ] If a guardian of my person is to be appointed, I nominate the agent acting under this power of attorney as guardian.

SUCCESSOR HEALTH CARE AGENT(S) (optional):

If the agent I selected is unable or does not want to make health care decisions for me, then I request the person(s) I name below to be my successor health care agent(s). Only one person at a time can serve as my agent (add another page if you want to add more successor agent names):

_____
(Successor agent #1 name, address and phone number)

_____
(Successor agent #2 name, address and phone number)

MY AGENT CAN MAKE HEALTH CARE DECISIONS FOR ME, INCLUDING:

    (i) Deciding to accept, withdraw, or decline treatment for any physical or mental condition of mine, including life-and-death decisions.
    (ii) Agreeing to admit me to or discharge me from any hospital, home, or other institution, including a mental health facility.
    (iii) Having complete access to my medical and mental health records, and sharing them with others as needed, including after I die.
    (iv) Carrying out the plans I have already made, or, if I have not done so, making decisions about my body or remains, including organ, tissue or whole body donation, autopsy, cremation, and burial.
    The above grant of power is intended to be as broad as possible so that my agent will have the authority to make any decision I could make to obtain or terminate any type of health care, including withdrawal of nutrition and hydration and other life-sustaining measures.

I AUTHORIZE MY AGENT TO (please check any one box):

[ ] Make decisions for me only when I cannot make them for myself. The physician(s) taking care of me will determine when I lack this ability.

    (If no box is checked, then the box above shall be implemented.) OR

[ ] Make decisions for me only when I cannot make them for myself. The physician(s) taking care of me will determine when I lack this ability. Starting now, for the purpose of assisting me with my health care plans and decisions, my agent shall have complete access to my medical and mental health records, the authority to share them with others as needed, and the complete ability to communicate with my personal physician(s) and other health care providers, including the ability to require an opinion of my physician as to whether I lack the ability to make decisions for myself. OR

[ ] Make decisions for me starting now and continuing after I am no longer able to make them for myself. While I am still able to make my own decisions, I can still do so if I want to.

The subject of life-sustaining treatment is of particular importance. Life-sustaining treatments may include tube feedings or fluids through a tube, breathing machines, and CPR. In general, in making decisions concerning life-sustaining treatment, your agent is instructed to consider the relief of suffering, the quality as well as the possible extension of your life, and your previously expressed wishes. Your agent will weigh the burdens versus benefits of proposed treatments in making decisions on your behalf.

Additional statements concerning the withholding or removal of life-sustaining treatment are described below. These can serve as a guide for your agent when making decisions for you. Ask your physician or health care provider if you have any questions about these statements.

SELECT ONLY ONE STATEMENT BELOW THAT BEST EXPRESSES YOUR WISHES (optional):

[ ] The quality of my life is more important than the length of my life. If I am unconscious and my attending physician believes, in accordance with reasonable medical standards, that I will not wake up or recover my ability to think, communicate with my family and friends, and experience my surroundings, I do not want treatments to prolong my life or delay my death, but I do want treatment or care to make me comfortable and to relieve me of pain.

[ ] Staying alive is more important to me, no matter how sick I am, how much I am suffering, the cost of the procedures, or how unlikely my chances for recovery are. I want my life to be prolonged to the greatest extent possible in accordance with reasonable medical standards.

SPECIFIC LIMITATIONS TO MY AGENT'S DECISION-MAKING AUTHORITY:

The above grant of power is intended to be as broad as possible so that your agent will have the authority to make any decision you could make to obtain or terminate any type of health care. If you wish to limit the scope of your agent's powers or prescribe special rules or limit the power to authorize autopsy or dispose of remains, you may do so specifically in this form.

_____

(attach additional lines or pages if needed).

SIGNATURE

My signature:_____   Today's date:_____

DELAYED REVOCATION

[   ] I elect to delay revocation of this power of attorney for 30 days after I communicate my intent to revoke it.

[   ] I elect for the revocation of this power of attorney to take effect immediately if I communicate my intent to revoke it.

WITNESS

HAVE YOUR WITNESS AGREE TO WHAT IS WRITTEN BELOW, AND THEN COMPLETE THE SIGNATURE PORTION:

I am at least 18 years old (check one of the options below):

[   ] I saw the principal sign this document, or

[   ] the principal told me that the signature or mark on the principal signature line is his or hers.

I am not the agent or successor agent(s) named in this document.

I am not related to the principal, the agent, or the successor agent(s) by blood, marriage, or adoption.

I am not the principal's physician, advanced practice registered nurse, dentist, podiatric physician, optometrist, psychologist, or a relative of one of those individuals.

I am not an owner or operator (or the relative of an owner or operator) of the health care facility where the principal is a patient or resident.

Witness Signature:_____   Witness printed name:_____

Witness address: _____

Today's date: _____

CHAPTER 11
FORM 5: LIVING WILL DECLARATION

IN FORM CAN REFUSE FURTHER MEDICAL CARE WHICH IS A SERIOUS ACTION

This form lets a person say to not give some health care if <u>later</u> their health is seen as very bad, and saying this in this form is a very serious action. This is a statutory form found in state law to use if wanted.

FORM SAYS IF PERSON GETS TERMINAL CONDITION TO STOP MOST CARE

This form <u>only applies if health later is very bad</u>, when (as form says) there is "incurable and irreversible injury, disease, or illness judged to be a terminal condition by my attending physician who has personally examined me and has determined that my death is imminent except for death delaying procedures". By law "terminal condition" means an "incurable and irreversible condition which is such that death is imminent and the application of death delaying procedures serves only to prolong the dying process".

When form applies <u>most health care will be stopped</u> and (as form says): "I direct that such procedures which would only prolong the dying process be withheld or withdrawn, and that I be permitted to die naturally with only the administration of … comfort care."

This form is often skipped and in recent years the Health Care Power Of Attorney more often is used. But some people like a Living Will to stress to family and doctors if health changes occur and their health gets bad later that unreasonable health care shouldn't be given.

FORM IS SIGNED BY PERSON DOING FORM AND THEN 2 WITNESSES

This form must be signed by person doing the form and 2 witnesses who must be at least age 18. A witness should a) not be entitled to a person's money or property if they die either by Illinois law or any known Will (so usually not spouse, child, or other close family of person), and b) not be legally responsible by law to pay for person's health care if needed (so usually not spouse or parent of person doing form). Using video-conference for "electronic signing" is now allowed but almost never done. The form once it is signed should be shown to all doctors and places that may be used to add it to medical files to follow. To cancel the form a person should tell Agent and probably tell people shown form to no longer follow it.

LIVING WILL DECLARATION

This declaration is made this ____ day of _____, 20___ (month, year). I, _____, being of sound mind, willfully and voluntarily make known my desires that my moment of death shall not be artificially postponed.

If at any time I should have an incurable and irreversible injury, disease, or illness judged to be a terminal condition by my attending physician who has personally examined me and has determined that my death is imminent except for death delaying procedures, I direct that such procedures which would only prolong the dying process be withheld or withdrawn, and that I be permitted to die naturally with only the administration of medication, sustenance, or the performance of any medical procedure deemed necessary by my attending physician to provide me with comfort care.

In the absence of my ability to give directions regarding the use of such death delaying procedures, it is my intention that this declaration shall be honored by my family and physician as the final expression of my legal right to refuse medical or surgical treatment and accept the consequences from such refusal.

DECLARANT

Declarant Signature: _____

City, County and State of Residence: _____

_____

WITNESSES

The declarant is personally known to me and I believe him or her to be of sound mind. I saw the declarant sign the declaration in my presence (or the declarant acknowledged in my presence that he or she had signed the declaration) and I signed the declaration as a witness in the presence of the declarant. I did not sign the declarant's signature above for or at the direction of the declarant. At the date of this instrument, I am not entitled to any portion of the estate of the declarant according to the laws of intestate succession or, to the best of my knowledge and belief, under any will of declarant or other instrument taking effect at declarant's death, or directly financially responsible for declarant's medical care.

Witness: _____ Witness: _____

CHAPTER 12
FORM 6: DO-NOT-RESUSCITATE

FORM STOPS SOME HEALTH CARE IMMEDIATELY WHICH IS A SERIOUS STEP

This form can say to <u>immediately</u> no longer try some health care listed in the form, like C.P.R. to try to help heart of breathing. Doing this in this form is a very serious action. This form is short so it can be read fast outside hospitals and other facilities like by paramedics who usually will ignore other health forms.

IN FORM CAN GIVE INSTRUCTIONS ON WHAT HEALTH CARE TO NOT GIVE

This form lets person say to <u>immediately</u> no longer try some health care listed in the form. In the form a person can specify some details about what health care to not give. Doctors often help fill out the form. The main thing done is to say not to give cardio-pulmonary resuscitation (C.P.R.) to attempt to restart heart or breathing, but there are is other health care a person can decline in form. Some places have their own form they prefer be used. Even after doing this form a person is usually free to override it, like by saying to paramedics or doctor, "I feel better and want C.P.R. and all care and please tear up D-N-R form on file."

FORM IS SIGNED BY A DOCTOR AND BY PERSON DOING THE FORM

The form must be signed by a doctor or similar health professional, and by person doing the form or someone on their behalf. Once signed the form should be shown to places and doctors giving care and made part of a person's medical file. Often a person keeps copies handy to show paramedics, EMTs, or other people who may want to give care, like on a bedside table, on home refrigerator (paramedics often look here), pinned to chest, in a pocket, or some people wear a " bracelet" or similar made by companies chosen by the state. To cancel the form person usually should tell people shown the form it is canceled.

HIPAA PERMITS DISCLOSURE OF DNR/POLST TO HEALTH CARE PROFESSIONALS AS NECESSARY FOR TREATMENT

State of Illinois
Illinois Department of Public Health

DO-NOT-RESUSCITATE (DNR)/PRACTITIONER ORDERS FOR LIFE-SUSTAINING TREATMENT (POLST) FORM

For patients, use of this form is completely voluntary. Follow these orders until changed. These medical orders are based on the patient's medical condition and preferences. Any section not completed does not invalidate the form and implies initiating all treatment for that section. With significant change of condition new orders may need to be written.

Patient Last Name	Patient First Name	MI
Date of Birth (mm/dd/yy)	Gender ❏ M ❏ F	
Address (street/city/state/ZIPcode)		

A — Check One
CARDIOPULMONARY RESUSCITATION (CPR) If patient has no pulse and is not breathing.
❏ Attempt Resuscitation/CPR   ❏ Do Not Attempt Resuscitation/DNR
(*Selecting CPR means **Full Treatment** in Section B is selected*)

When not in cardiopulmonary arrest, follow orders B and C.

B — Check One (optional)
MEDICAL INTERVENTIONS If patient is found with a pulse and/or is breathing.

❏ **Full Treatment: Primary goal of sustaining life by medically indicated means.** In addition to treatment described in Selective Treatment and Comfort-Focused Treatment, use intubation, mechanical ventilation and cardioversion as indicated. *Transfer to hospital and/or intensive care unit if indicated.*

❏ **Selective Treatment: Primary goal of treating medical conditions with selected medical measures.** In addition to treatment described in Comfort-Focused Treatment, use medical treatment, IV fluids and IV medications (may include antibiotics and vasopressors), as medically appropriate and consistent with patient preference. Do Not Intubate. May consider less invasive airway support (e.g. CPAP, BiPAP). *Transfer to hospital, if indicated. Generally avoid the intensive care unit.*

❏ **Comfort-Focused Treatment: Primary goal of maximizing comfort.** Relieve pain and suffering through the use of medication by any route as needed; use oxygen, suctioning and manual treatment of airway obstruction. Do not use treatments listed in Full and Selective Treatment unless consistent with comfort goal. *Request transfer to hospital only if comfort needs cannot be met in current location.*

Optional Additional Orders _____

C — Check One (optional)
MEDICALLY ADMINISTERED NUTRITION (if medically indicated) Offer food by mouth, if feasible and as desired.
❏ Long-term medically administered nutrition, including feeding tubes.
❏ Trial period of medically administered nutrition, including feeding tubes.
❏ No medically administered means of nutrition, including feeding tubes.

Additional Instructions (e.g., length of trial period)
_____
_____

D
DOCUMENTATION OF DISCUSSION (Check all appropriate boxes below)
❏ Patient   ❏ Agent under health care power of attorney
❏ Parent of minor   ❏ Health care surrogate decision maker (See Page 2 for priority list)

Signature of Patient or Legal Representative

Signature (required)	Name (print)	Date

Signature of Witness to Consent (Witness required for a valid form)
I am 18 years of age or older and acknowledge the above person has had an opportunity to read this form and have witnessed the giving of consent by the above person or the above person has acknowledged his/her signature or mark on this form in my presence.

Signature (required)	Name (print)	Date

E
Signature of Attending Practitioner (physician, licensed resident (second year or higher), advanced practice nurse or physician assistant)
My signature below indicates to the best of my knowledge and belief that these orders are consistent with the patient's medical condition and preferences.

Print Attending Practitioner Name (required)	Phone ( ) ____ - _____
Attending Practitioner Signature (required)	Date (required)

Page 1

Form Revision Date January 2015   (Prior form versions are also valid.)

SEND A COPY OF FORM WITH PATIENT WHENEVER TRANSFERRED OR DISCHARGED • COPY ON ANY COLOR OF PAPER IS ACCEPTABLE • 2015

HIPAA PERMITS DISCLOSURE OF DNR/POLST TO HEALTH CARE PROFESSIONALS AS NECESSARY FOR TREATMENT

THIS SIDE FOR INFORMATIONAL PURPOSES ONLY

Patient Last Name	Patient First Name	MI

The Illinois Department of Public Health (IDPH) Do Not Resuscitate (DNR)/Practitioner Orders for Life Sustaining Treatment (POLST) **is always voluntary**. This order records your wishes for medical treatment in your current state of health. Once initial medical treatment is begun and the risks and benefits of further therapy are clear, your treatment wishes may change. Your medical care and this form can be changed to reflect your new wishes at any time. However, no form can address all the medical treatment decisions that may need to be made. The Power of Attorney for Health Care Advance Directive form (POAHC) is recommended for all capable adults, regardless of their health status. A POAHC allows you to document, in detail, your future health care instructions and name a Legal Representative to speak for you if you are unable to speak for yourself.

Advance Directive Information

I also have the following advance directives (OPTIONAL)

❏ Health Care Power of Attorney   ❏ Living Will Declaration   ❏ Mental Health Treatment Preference Declaration

Contact Person Name	Contact Phone Number

Health Care Professional Information

Preparer Name	Phone Number
Preparer Title	Date Prepared

Completing the IDPH Do Not Resuscitate (DNR)/POLST Form
- **The completion of a DNR/POLST form is always voluntary, cannot be mandated and may be changed at any time.**
- A DNR/POLST should reflect current preferences of persons completing the DNR/POLST Form; encourage completion of a POAHC.
- Verbal/phone orders are acceptable with follow-up signature by attending physician in accordance with facility/community policy.
- Use of original form is encouraged. Photocopies and faxes on any color of paper also are legal and valid forms.

Reviewing a Do Not Resuscitate (DNR)/POLST Form
This DNR/POLST form should be reviewed periodically and if:
- The patient is transferred from one care setting or care level to another,
- or there is a substantial change in the patient's health status,
- or the patient's treatment preferences change,
- or the patient's primary care professional changes.

Voiding or revoking a Do Not Resuscitate (DNR)/POLST Form
- A patient with capacity can void or revoke the form, and/or request alternative treatment.
- Changing, modifying or revising a DNR/POLST form requires completion of a new DNR/POLST form.
- Draw line through sections A through E and write "VOID" across page if any DNR/POLST form is replaced or becomes invalid. Beneath the written "VOID" write in the date of change and re-sign.
- If included in an electronic medical record, follow all voiding procedures of facility.

Illinois Health Care Surrogate Act (755 ILCS 40/25) Priority Order
1. Patient's guardian of person
2. Patient's spouse or partner of a registered civil union
3. Adult child
4. Parent
5. Adult sibling
6. Adult grandchild
7. A close friend of the patient
8. The patient's guardian of the estate

For more information, visit the IDPH Statement of Illinois law at
http://www.idph.state.il.us/public/books/advin.htm

HIPAA (HEALTH INSURANCE PORTABILITY AND ACCOUNTABILITY ACT of 1996) PERMITS DISCLOSURE TO HEALTH CARE PROFESSIONALS AS NECESSARY FOR TREATMENT

IOCI 15-464

SEND A COPY OF FORM WITH PATIENT WHENEVER TRANSFERRED OR DISCHARGED • COPY ON ANY COLOR OF PAPER IS ACCEPTABLE • 2015

CHAPTER 13
FORM 7: STATUTORY SHORT FORM
POWER OF ATTORNEY FOR PROPERTY

FORM LETS POWER BE GIVEN OVER PROPERTY, MONEY, AND MORE

This form lets a person give power to someone to let them do things with the person's money, property, debt, and more. Some people call this a "Financial Power Of Attorney". This is a statutory form found in state law to use if people want. This form is called "durable" since it still has power if a person doing the form is later incapacitated, but power of the form ends at their death.

FORM GIVES POWER TO LET SOMEONE HELP WITH PROPERTY AND MONEY

This form lets person doing the form, the "Principal", give power to someone, the "Attorney-in-Fact" or "Agent", over money, property, and more. Often named Agent is a trusted person like a spouse or friend. This form can let the Agent do things like pay bills, move money in accounts, buy or sell things, get records, borrow, and sign contracts for the Principal. This can help if a person is sick, busy, or away, and may avoid need for a nursing home, guardian, or conservator. A person till incapacitated can overrule or fire an Agent. Powers given by the form can be picked but most people give most powers so a bank or other party won't think not enough power was given to do something. Most people skip naming a "Successor Agent" since this is rarely needed. Many people put today's date for when the form starts and put "never" for when it ends. When an Agent signs it should be like, "Ed Doe signing as Agent under Power of Attorney for Ann Po".

DUE TO RISKS INCLUDING FRAUD MANY SKIP FORM OR CONSULT A LAWYER

Using this form can be risky and lead to loss of money and property since the Agent can do harmful things like buy unneeded or costly items, embezzle or steal, or allow other people to steal. Agents have a duty to act reasonably for Principal but may might be out of money later so can't pay to undo their harm. Usually banks or others can't be blamed for obeying an Agent, and if they hesitate to obey they may even owe a small penalty. The law is complex and basic acts may be fine like paying bills, getting records, moving funds, but other acts may be improper like gifts to anyone, risky investments, or uncommon things. It is best if a person not their Agent do anything unusual. Many people skip the form or first see a lawyer.

PERSON SIGNS FORM WITH NOTARY AND WITH 1 OR 2 WITNESSES

This form must be signed by person doing the form and 1 witness in front of a notary, but most states require 2 witnesses so this is common even in Illinois. A witness must a) be at least 18, b) not Agent or Successor Agent in form or their spouse, c) not employee, owner, or tied to hospital or any place giving care, and d) not parent, brother, sister, child, or grandchild of person doing form (or spouse of any of these). The form has a Notice page for person doing the form to initial, and at form end is a Notice page for Agent. Near end of the form is option for Agent to later write an example "specimen signature". The very last page in this Chapter is an "Agent's Certification" which later some banks may ask be signed by the Agent. To cancel the form a person should tell Agent and take back copies and maybe tell people shown the form.

NOTICE TO THE INDIVIDUAL SIGNING THE ILLINOIS STATUTORY SHORT FORM POWER OF ATTORNEY FOR PROPERTY

PLEASE READ THIS NOTICE CAREFULLY. The form that you will be signing is a legal document. It is governed by the Illinois Power of Attorney Act. If there is anything about this form that you do not understand, you should ask a lawyer to explain it to you.

The purpose of this Power of Attorney is to give your designated "agent" broad powers to handle your financial affairs, which may include the power to pledge, sell, or dispose of any of your real or personal property, even without your consent or any advance notice to you. When using the Statutory Short Form, you may name successor agents, but you may not name co-agents.

This form does not impose a duty upon your agent to handle your financial affairs, so it is important that you select an agent who will agree to do this for you. It is also important to select an agent whom you trust, since you are giving that agent control over your financial assets and property. Any agent who does act for you has a duty to act in good faith for your benefit and to use due care, competence, and diligence. He or she must also act in accordance with the law and with the directions in this form. Your agent must keep a record of all receipts, disbursements, and significant actions taken as your agent.

Unless you specifically limit the period of time that this Power of Attorney will be in effect, your agent may exercise the powers given to him or her throughout your lifetime, both before and after you become incapacitated. A court, however, can take away the powers of your agent if it finds that the agent is not acting properly. You may also revoke this Power of Attorney if you wish.

This Power of Attorney does not authorize your agent to appear in court for you as an attorney-at-law or otherwise to engage in the practice of law unless he or she is a licensed attorney who is authorized to practice law in Illinois.

The powers you give your agent are explained more fully in Section 3-4 of the Illinois Power of Attorney Act. This form is a part of that law. The "NOTE" paragraphs throughout this form are instructions.

You are not required to sign this Power of Attorney, but it will not take effect without your signature. You should not sign this Power of Attorney if you do not understand everything in it, and what your agent will be able to do if you do sign it.

Please place your initials on the following line indicating that you have read this Notice:

Principal's initials:_____

ILLINOIS STATUTORY SHORT FORM POWER OF ATTORNEY FOR PROPERTY

1. I, _____,
_____(insert name and address of **principal**) hereby revoke all prior powers of attorney for property executed by me and appoint:
_____
(insert name and address of agent) (NOTE: You may not name co-agents using this form.)

as my **attorney-in-fact (my "agent")** to act for me and in my name (in any way I could act in person) with respect to **the following powers**, as defined in Section 3-4 of the "Statutory Short Form Power of Attorney for Property Law" (including all amendments), but subject to any limitations on or additions to the specified powers inserted in paragraph 2 or 3 below:

(NOTE: You must strike out any one or more of the following categories of powers you do not want your agent to have. Failure to strike the title of any category will cause the powers described in that category to be granted to the agent. To strike out a category you must draw a line through the title of that category.)

(a) Real estate transactions.
(b) Financial institution transactions.
(c) Stock and bond transactions.
(d) Tangible personal property transactions.
(e) Safe deposit box transactions.
(f) Insurance and annuity transactions.
(g) Retirement plan transactions.
(h) Social Security, employment and military service benefits.
(i) Tax matters.
(j) Claims and litigation.
(k) Commodity and option transactions.
(l) Business operations.
(m) Borrowing transactions.
(n) Estate transactions.
(o) All other property transactions.

(NOTE: Limitations on and additions to the agent's powers may be included in this power of attorney if they are specifically described below.)

2. The powers granted above shall not include the following powers or shall be modified or limited in the following particulars:

(NOTE: Here you may include any specific limitations you deem appropriate, such as a prohibition or conditions on the sale of particular stock or real estate or special rules on borrowing by the agent.)

_____
_____
_____
_____

3. In addition to the powers granted above, I grant my agent the following powers:

(NOTE: Here you may add any other delegable powers including, without limitation, power to make gifts, exercise powers of appointment, name or change beneficiaries or joint tenants or revoke or amend any trust specifically referred to below.)

_____
_____
_____
_____

(NOTE: Your agent will have authority to employ other persons as necessary to enable the agent to properly exercise the powers granted in this form, but your agent will have to make all discretionary decisions. If you want to give your agent the right to delegate discretionary decision-making powers to others, you should keep paragraph 4, otherwise it should be struck out.)

4. My agent shall have the right by written instrument to delegate any or all of the foregoing powers involving discretionary decision-making to any person or persons whom my agent may select, but such delegation may be amended or revoked by any agent (including any successor) named by me who is acting under this power of attorney at the time of reference.

(NOTE: Your agent will be entitled to reimbursement for all reasonable expenses incurred in acting under this power of attorney. Strike out paragraph 5 if you do not want your agent to also be entitled to reasonable compensation for services as agent.)

5. My agent shall be entitled to reasonable compensation for services rendered as agent under this power of attorney.

(NOTE: This power of attorney may be amended or revoked by you at any time and in any manner. Absent amendment or revocation, the authority granted in this power of attorney will become effective at the time this power is signed and will continue until your death, unless a limitation on the beginning date or duration is made by initialing and completing one or both of paragraphs 6 and 7.)

6. This power of attorney shall become effective on _____.

(NOTE: Insert a future date or event during your lifetime, such as a court determination of your disability or a written determination by your physician that you are incapacitated, when you want this power to first take effect.)

7. This power of attorney shall terminate on _____.

(NOTE: Insert a future date or event, such as a court determination that you are not under a legal disability or a written determination by your physician that you are not incapacitated, if you want this power to terminate prior to your death.)

(NOTE: If you wish to name one or more successor agents, insert the name and address of each successor agent in paragraph 8.)

8. If any agent named by me shall die, become incompetent, resign or refuse to accept the office of agent, I name the following (each to act alone and successively, in the order named) as successor(s) to such agent: _____
_____.

For purposes of this paragraph 8, a person shall be considered to be incompetent if and while the person is a minor or an adjudicated incompetent or a person with a disability or the person is unable to give prompt and intelligent consideration to business matters, as certified by a licensed physician.

(NOTE: If you wish to, you may name your agent as guardian of your estate if a court decides that one should be appointed. To do this, retain paragraph 9, and the court will appoint your agent if the court finds that this appointment will serve your best interests and welfare. Strike out paragraph 9 if you do not want your agent to act as guardian.)

9. If a guardian of my estate (my property) is to be appointed, I nominate the agent acting under this power of attorney as such guardian, to serve without bond or security.

10. I am fully informed as to all the contents of this form and understand the full import of this grant of powers to my agent.

(NOTE: This form does not authorize your agent to appear in court for you as an attorney-at-law or otherwise to engage in the practice of law unless he or she is a licensed attorney who is authorized to practice law in Illinois.)

11. The Notice to Agent is incorporated by reference and included as part of this form.

Dated: _____   Signed: _____
                                                       (principal)

(NOTE: This power of attorney will not be effective unless it is signed by at least one witness and your signature is notarized, using the form below. The notary may not also sign as a witness.)

The undersigned witness certifies that _____, known to me to be the same person whose name is subscribed as principal to the foregoing power of attorney, appeared before me and the notary public and acknowledged signing and delivering the instrument as the free and voluntary act of the principal, for the uses and purposes therein set forth. I believe him or her to be of sound mind and memory. The undersigned witness also certifies that the witness is not:

(a) the attending physician or mental health service provider or a relative of the physician or provider;

(b) an owner, operator, or relative of an owner or operator of a health care facility in which the principal is a patient or resident;

(c) a parent, sibling, descendant, or any spouse of such parent, sibling, or descendant of either the principal or any agent or successor agent under the foregoing power of attorney, whether such relationship is by blood, marriage, or adoption; or

(d) an agent or successor agent under the foregoing power of attorney.

Dated: _____ Signed: _____
                                              (witness)

(NOTE: Illinois requires <u>only one witness</u>, but other jurisdictions may require more than one witness. If you wish to have a second witness, have him or her certify and sign here:)

(Second witness) The undersigned witness certifies that _____, known to me to be the same person whose name is subscribed as principal to the foregoing power of attorney, appeared before me and the notary public and acknowledged signing and delivering the instrument as the free and voluntary act of the principal, for the uses and purposes therein set forth. I believe him or her to be of sound mind and memory. The undersigned witness also certifies that the witness is not:

(a) the attending physician or mental health service provider or a relative of the physician or provider;

(b) an owner, operator, or relative of an owner or operator of a health care facility in which the principal is a patient or resident;

(c) a parent, sibling, descendant, or any spouse of such parent, sibling, or descendant of either the principal or any agent or successor agent under the foregoing power of attorney, whether such relationship is by blood, marriage, or adoption; or

(d) an agent or successor agent under the foregoing power of attorney.

Dated: _____ Signed: _____
                                              (witness)

State of _____)
) SS.
County of _____)

    The undersigned, a notary public in and for the above county and state, certifies that _____, known to me to be the same person whose name is subscribed as principal to the foregoing power of attorney, appeared before me and the witness(es) _____ (and _____) in person and acknowledged signing and delivering the instrument as the free and voluntary act of the principal, for the uses and purposes therein set forth (, and certified to the correctness of the signature(s) of the agent(s)).

Dated: _____ Signed: _____
                                                         (notary public)
                                          My commission expires _____

(NOTE: You may, but are not required to, request your agent and successor agents to provide <u>specimen signatures</u> below. If you include specimen signatures in this power of attorney, you must complete the certification opposite the signatures of the agents.)

Specimen signatures of agent (and successors)	I certify that the signatures of my agent (and successors) are genuine.
_____ (agent)	_____ (principal)
_____ (successor agent)	_____ (principal)
_____ (successor agent)	_____ (principal)

(NOTE: The name, address, and phone number of the person preparing this form or who assisted the principal in completing this form should be inserted below.)

Name: _____
Address: _____
Phone: _____

NOTICE TO AGENT

When you accept the authority granted under this power of attorney a special legal relationship, known as agency, is created between you and the principal. Agency imposes upon you duties that continue until you resign or the power of attorney is terminated or revoked.

As agent you must:

(1) do what you know the principal reasonably expects you to do with the principal's property;

(2) act in good faith for the best interest of the principal, using due care, competence, and diligence;

(3) keep a complete and detailed record of all receipts, disbursements, and significant actions conducted for the principal;

(4) attempt to preserve the principal's estate plan, to the extent actually known by the agent, if preserving the plan is consistent with the principal's best interest; and

(5) cooperate with a person who has authority to make health care decisions for the principal to carry out the principal's reasonable expectations to the extent actually in the principal's best interest.

As agent you must not do any of the following:

(1) act so as to create a conflict of interest that is inconsistent with the other principles in this Notice to Agent;

(2) do any act beyond the authority granted in this power of attorney;

(3) commingle the principal's funds with your funds;

(4) borrow funds or other property from the principal, unless otherwise authorized;

(5) continue acting on behalf of the principal if you learn of any event that terminates this power of attorney or your authority under this power of attorney, such as the death of the principal, your legal separation from the principal, or the dissolution of your marriage to the principal.

If you have special skills or expertise, you must use those special skills and expertise when acting for the principal.

You must disclose your identity as an agent whenever you act for the principal by writing or printing the name of the principal and signing your own name "as Agent" in the following manner: **"(Principal's Name) by (Your Name) as Agent"** .

The meaning of the powers granted to you is contained in Section 3-4 of the Illinois Power of Attorney Act, which is incorporated by reference into the body of the power of attorney for property document.

If you violate your duties as agent or act outside the authority granted to you, you may be liable for any damages, including attorney's fees and costs, caused by your violation.

If there is anything about this document or your duties that you do not understand, you should seek legal advice from an attorney.

AGENT'S CERTIFICATION AND ACCEPTANCE OF AUTHORITY
(OPTIONAL AND DONE LATER WHEN REQUESTED BY THIRD PARTY)

I, _____ (insert name of agent), certify that the attached is a true copy of a power of attorney naming the undersigned as agent or successor agent for _____ (insert name of principal).

I certify that to the best of my knowledge the principal had the capacity to execute the power of attorney, is alive, and has not revoked the power of attorney; that my powers as agent have not been altered or terminated; and that the power of attorney remains in full force and effect.

I accept appointment as agent under this power of attorney.

This certification and acceptance is made under penalty of perjury.*

Dated: _____

_____
(Agent's Signature)

_____
(Print Agent's Name)

_____
(Agent's Address)

*(NOTE: Perjury is defined in Section 32-2 of the Criminal Code of 1961, and is a Class 3 felony.)

CHAPTER 14
FORM 8: APPOINTMENT OF SHORT-TERM GUARDIAN (FOR MINOR CHILD)

FORM LETS PARENT GIVE POWER TO SOMEONE OVER MINOR CHILD

This form lets a parent give someone power over minor child under 18. This is a statutory form found in state law to use if wanted. The Illinois Department of Children and Family Services has a nice online version of this form that filled in online and then printed.

FORM LETS PARENT GIVE SOMEONE POWER OVER CHILD UNDER 18

A parent (or a guardian) with a minor child under 18 can do this form to give to a person they name as "Short-Term Guardian" power over a child's health care, school, discipline, and more (but not marriage, adoption, property, or money). The person doing this form can overrule or fire the Guardian at any time. The person who is Guardian should be a U.S. resident, at least 18, and usually have no felony conviction. This form is sometimes used if a parent or child is away from the other for work, school, sports, drug treatment, prison or jail, immigration, military, month long visit with family or friends, or if child is sick in hospital and needs a person close by to make quick decisions. The form is not usually done for minor situations like babysitter, daycare, week with relative, or any cases where a parent can come fast. Using this form may avoid need for serious legal action like legal guardianship or change of custody. The form is good for maximum of 365 days or end of any military deployment then it must be re-done.

PARENT SIGNS FORM WITH 2 WITNESSES AND LATER 2ND PARENT SIGNS

To complete the form at least 1 parent (or guardian) signs it with 2 witnesses who then sign it too. The 2nd parent usually signs either in a) the main signature area to show they are fully comfortable with the person chosen as Guardian or b) as "consenting parent" to show they do not object. As the form says in some cases a 2nd parent needn't sign. The Guardian later must sign the form before they use it. Witnesses can be anyone at least 18 and not named Guardian in the form. The law explaining this form does say if 2nd parent offers to and can watch a child it is usually best if they be allowed to do this. Some people show the form quickly to doctors, schools, and similar to make clear it might be used later. To cancel the form a parent just tells Guardian, takes back copies, and maybe tells any places shown the form to no longer follow it.

APPOINTMENT OF SHORT-TERM GUARDIAN (FOR MINOR CHILD)

IT IS IMPORTANT TO READ THE FOLLOWING INSTRUCTIONS:

By properly completing this form, a parent or the guardian of the person of the child is appointing a guardian of a child of the parent (or a minor ward of the guardian, as the case may be) for a period of up to 365 days. A separate form should be completed for each child. The person appointed as the guardian must sign the form, but need not do so at the same time as the parent or parents or guardian.

If you are a parent or guardian who is a member of the Armed Forces of the United States, including any reserve component thereof, or the commissioned corps of the National Oceanic and Atmospheric Administration or the Public Health Service of the United States Department of Health and Human Services detailed by proper authority for duty with the Armed Forces of the United States, or who is required to enter or serve in the active military service of the United States under a call or order of the President of the United States or to serve on State active duty, you may appoint a short-term guardian for your child for the period of your active duty service plus 30 days. When executing this form, include the date your active duty service is scheduled to begin in part 3 and the date your active duty service is scheduled to end in part 4.

This form may not be used to appoint a guardian if there is a guardian already appointed for the child, except that if a guardian of the person of the child has been appointed, that guardian may use this form to appoint a short-term guardian. Both living parents of a child may together appoint a guardian of the child, or the guardian of the person of the child may appoint a guardian of the child, for a period of up to 365 days through the use of this form. If the short-term guardian is appointed by both living parents of the child, the parents need not sign the form at the same time.

1. Parent (or guardian) and Child. I, _____, currently residing at _____, am a parent (or the guardian of the person) of the following child (or of a child likely to be born): _____ .

2. Guardian. I hereby appoint the following person as the short-term guardian for the child: _____ .

3. Effective date. This appointment becomes effective: (check one if you wish it to be applicable)
    ( ) On the date that I state in writing that I am no longer either willing or able to make and carry out day-to-day child care decisions concerning the child.
    ( ) On the date that a physician familiar with my condition certifies in writing that I am no longer willing or able to make and carry out day-to-day child care decisions concerning the child.
    ( ) On the date that I am admitted as an in-patient to a hospital or other health care institution.
    ( ) On the following date: _____.
    ( ) On the date my active duty service begins: _____.
    ( ) Upon an administrative separation, as defined in Section 11-1.
    ( ) Other: _____.

[NOTE: If this item is not completed, the appointment is effective immediately upon the date the form is signed and dated below.]

4. Termination. This appointment shall terminate 365 days after the effective date, unless it terminates as determined by the event or date I have indicated below: (check one if you wish it to be applicable)
    ( ) On the date that I state in writing that I am willing and able to make and carry out day-to-day child care decisions concerning the child, but not more than 365 days after the effective date.
    ( ) On the date that a physician familiar with my condition certifies in writing that I am willing and able to make and carry out day-to-day child care decisions concerning the child, but not more than 365 days after the effective date.
    ( ) On the date that I am discharged from the hospital or other health care institution where I was admitted as an in-patient, which established the effective date, but not more than 365 days after the effective date.
    ( ) On the date which is (state a number of days, but no more than 365 days) days after the effective date.
    ( ) On the date no more than 30 days after my active duty service is scheduled to end: (insert date active duty service is scheduled to end).
    ( ) In the event the administrative separation, as defined in Section 11-1, has been resolved.
    ( ) Other: _____.

[NOTE: If this item is not completed, the appointment will be effective for a period of 365 days, beginning on the effective date.]

5. Date and signature of appointing parent or guardian. This appointment is made this _____ day of _____, 20_____.

        Signed: _____

                _____
                (appointing parents or guardians)

6. Witnesses. I saw the parent (or the guardian of the person of the child) sign this instrument or I saw the parent (or the guardian of the person of the child) direct someone to sign this instrument for the parent (or the guardian). Then I signed this instrument as a witness in the presence of the parent (or the guardian). I am not appointed in this instrument to act as the short-term guardian for the child.

Witness signature:_____ Printed name:_____

Witness address:_____

Witness signature:_____ Printed name:_____

Witness address:_____

7. Acceptance of short-term guardian. I accept this appointment as short-term guardian on this _____ day of _____, 20_____.

        Signed: _____
                (short-term guardian)

8. Consent of child's other parent. I, _____, currently residing at _____, hereby consent to this appointment on this _____ day of _____, 20_____.

        Signed: _____
                (consenting parent)

[NOTE: The signature of a consenting parent is unneeded if one of these apply:
(i) the child's other parent has died; or
(ii) the whereabouts of the child's other parent are not known; or
(iii) the child's other parent is not willing or able to make and carry out day-to-day child care decisions concerning the child; or
(iv) the child's parents were never married and no court has issued an order establishing parentage.]

CHAPTER 15
FORM 9: APPOINTMENT OF AGENT TO CONTROL DISPOSITION OF REMAINS

LETS PERSON BE NAMED TO CONTROL FUNERAL AND ANY CREMATION

This form lets a person be named to control a dead person's remains and all related things like the funeral, ceremonies, burial, cremation, and buying things to do all this. This is a statutory form.

IN FORM CAN NAME AGENT TO CONTROL FUNERAL AND RELATED MATTERS

In the form an "Agent" can be named to control a person's dead body and related issues like funeral, burial, cremation, and what to buy for all this. The word "appointment" is in the form's title since this just means to name someone to do a job. Naming more people to be Agent if needed ("Successors") is often skipped since it is rarely needed. If this form is not done by law control of all this is by closest family (spouse, children, parents, then siblings). People use the form rarely usually only if it seems family may be too upset while mourning, be bad with money, or do unwanted things. Payment for things comes from pre-paid funeral accounts, insurance, and dead person's or estate's money and property, and Executor and family legally must help Agent arrange payment with these. The form has an area for directions that Agent and family must follow, but often a person skips this and trusts everyone to do what discussed or mentioned. Legally people including family should do the funeral, burial, and related things the dead person wanted if their properly, money, and estate can afford it.

SEVERAL OPTIONS ABOUT BODILY REMAINS AND EVENTS EXIST

After a death a funeral home or crematorium usually comes get the body. About half of people pick burial and half cremation. If doing cremation the "cremains" go to family or "columbarium" vault in cemetery.

Half of people do not do early events in first month when shocked family may be unready for visitors. Importantly, if "Direct Burial" or "Direct Cremation" is requested costs may be 80% off usual $10,000+ but this skips events with body till burial or cremation in done with no family involvement. Weeks later people may do ash scattering, ceremony, or dinner at park, house, church, or hall, often with food, speech, or video.

Half of people do early events within month, and there are many options for a person to pick from. First, some people do within days a "Vigil", "Viewing", or "Wake", where family and friends talk or just pray maybe in room with body (closed or open casket) or cremated ashes, often at Funeral Home or church. Second, some people do big ceremony within week of either a) funeral (maybe with Mass) in church with priest or minister, or b) informal event like "Celebration of Life" or "Remembrance" with or without the body. Third, some people do final event at cemetery (religious or not), like a burial or putting ashes in a vault.

FORM IS SIGNED BY PERSON IN FRONT OF A NOTARY

This form is signed by person doing the form in front of a notary who then notarizes it. Later before using the form the Agent must sign it too. The form should be kept so it's found quickly within days of death, or it can be immediately given to Agent to hold. The form can be canceled by telling Agent and usually anyone else shown the form it is canceled.

APPOINTMENT OF AGENT TO CONTROL DISPOSITION OF REMAINS
(755 Illinois Compiled Statutes 65/10)

I, _____, being of sound mind, willfully and voluntarily make known my desire that, upon my death, the disposition of my remains shall be controlled by _____ (name of agent first named below) and, with respect to that subject only, I hereby appoint such person as my agent (attorney-in-fact). All decisions made by my agent with respect to the disposition of my remains, including cremation, shall be binding.

SPECIAL DIRECTIONS:
Set forth below are any special directions limiting the power granted to my agent:

_____
_____
_____
_____
_____
_____
_____

If the disposition of my remains is by cremation, then:
( ) I do not wish to allow any of my survivors the option of canceling my cremation and selecting alternative arrangements, regardless of whether my survivors deem a change to be appropriate.
( ) I wish to allow only the survivors I have designated below the option of canceling my cremation and selecting alternative arrangements, if they deem a change to be appropriate:
_____
_____

ASSUMPTION:
THE AGENT, AND EACH SUCCESSOR AGENT, BY ACCEPTING THIS APPOINTMENT, AGREES TO AND ASSUMES THE OBLIGATIONS PROVIDED HEREIN. AN **AGENT MAY SIGN AT ANY TIME**, BUT AN AGENT'S AUTHORITY TO ACT IS NOT EFFECTIVE UNTIL THE AGENT SIGNS BELOW TO INDICATE THE ACCEPTANCE OF APPOINTMENT. ANY NUMBER OF AGENTS MAY SIGN, BUT ONLY THE SIGNATURE OF THE AGENT ACTING AT ANY TIME IS REQUIRED.

AGENT:
Name: _____ Phone: _____
Address: _____
Signature Indicating Acceptance of Appointment: _____
Date of Signature: _____

SUCCESSORS:
If my agent dies, becomes legally disabled, resigns, or refuses to act, I hereby appoint the following persons (each to act alone and successively, in the order named) to serve as my agent (attorney-in-fact) to control the disposition of my remains as authorized by this document:

1. First Successor
   Name: _____ Phone: _____
   Address: _____
   Signature Indicating Acceptance of Appointment: _____
   Date of Signature: _____

2. Second Successor
   Name: _____ Phone: _____
   Address: _____
   Signature Indicating Acceptance of Appointment: _____
   Date of Signature: _____

DURATION:
This appointment becomes effective upon my death.

PRIOR APPOINTMENTS REVOKED:
I hereby revoke any prior appointment of any person to control the disposition of my remains.

RELIANCE:
I hereby agree that any hospital, cemetery organization, business operating a crematory or columbarium or both, funeral director or embalmer, or funeral establishment who receives a copy of this document may act under it. Any modification or revocation of this document is not effective as to any such party until that party receives actual notice of the modification or revocation. No such party shall be liable because of reliance on a copy of this document.

Signed this _____ day of _____, 20____.

Signature: _____

STATE OF ILLINOIS
COUNTY OF _____

BEFORE ME, the undersigned, a Notary Public, on this day personally appeared _____, proved to me on the basis of satisfactory evidence to be the person whose name is subscribed to the foregoing instrument and acknowledged to me that he/she executed the same for the purposes and consideration therein expressed.

Given under my hand and seal of office this _____ day of _____, 20____.

Notary Signature: _____
Printed Name: _____
Notary Public, State of Illinois, Commission Expires: _____

APPENDIX: SAMPLE FILLED OUT FORMS

TO GET FORMS TO USE PEOPLE CAN:

(1) PHOTOCOPY BOOK PAGES,

(2) TEAR OUT PAGES FROM A BOOK, OR

(3) DOWNLOAD BOOK WITH FORMS FROM WWW.DAVENPORTPUBLISHING.COM AND USUALLY PDF FORM AT IS BEST TO AVOID SPACING/FORMAT CHANGES, AND THEN PEOPLE JUST HANDWRITE ON THE PRINTED OUT DOCUMENT.

EMAIL ANY COMMENTS TO DAVENPORTPRESS@GMAIL.COM .

On the next pages to show how it can be done are some sample filled out legal forms.

People can add words to legal forms by computer or typewriter to be neater, but many people just by hand use pen, marker, or pencil to handwrite words into forms.

It is not required but is bit better if signatures are in ink or marker not pencil.

Many parts of the forms especially Will gifts can be left empty and unfilled.

Anyone can fill in words in legal form not just the person doing the form, like a friend with neat writing can fill in all the words, addresses, and dates that are needed. Only the final signatures must be done by each person who wants the form.

To add words in form by pen, pencil, typewriter, or computer any of these is fine:
"I appoint ___*John Doe*___ as Agent",
"I appoint ___John Doe___ as Agent",
"I appoint John Doe as Agent".

When doing forms it may help to know "respectively" means "in order just stated".

People need not worry about neatness or small mistakes, and a document is usually fine if those people who knew a decedent in life can tell the likely meaning.

Sample Filled Out Form: Last Will and Testament (Standard)

LAST WILL AND TESTAMENT

I, __Susan Lee Maxwell__, of __Lake__ County, Illinois, do revoke all prior Wills, Testaments, and Codicils, and do make, publish, and declare this as my Will. When doing this I am of sound mind and under no duress or undue influence.

1. GIFTS. I give these gifts but to get a gift the recipient must survive the Testator, except as otherwise stated below.

SKIPPED

I give _____ to _____.

I give _____ to _____.

I give _____ to _____.

I give _____ to _____.

I give _____ to _____.

I give _____ to _____.

I give _____ to _____.

I give _____ to _____.

I give _____ to _____.

I give _____ to _____.

2. RESIDUE. I give the rest and residue and remainder of my estate, my property of any kind and nature, and anything I have an interest in (all of which is called the "residue"), so long as any such thing was not transferred by other Will provisions, as follows:

 a) to __Paul Thomas Maxwell__ who survive me with persons just named who survive me taking the share of non-survivors, then

 b) to __Jennifer Pamela Maxwell and Oscar Kent__ and if any of those just named do not survive me their part goes to their lineal descendants, per stirpes.

3. ADMINISTRATION. I name and appoint _Paul Thomas Maxwell_ as Executor including for me, my Will, and my estate.

4. MISCELLANEOUS. The following applies to this Will and generally.

Priority of Will gifts of the same type is based on the order they are written.

The words "give" and "gift" also means a devise, bequest, grant, legacy, or similar.

If gift or gift section mentions survival, survive, or surviving then survival is an absolute condition and anti-lapse laws or similar have no effect.

In this document no unfilled part is a mistake and residue spaces may be left blank.

Any failure to make gifts to family including children is intentional and not a mistake.

No gift or transfer made during life reduces or offsets a Will gift unless during my life I expressly called it a "loan" or "advancement".

Use of particular gender shall include other genders, reference to singular or plural shall be interchangeable, and "they" may be singular or plural.

If context permits the terms Executor, Personal Representative, and Administrator shall be seen as interchangeable as if all were written, and if context permits Guardian of the Estate is interchangeable with Guardian of the Property and with Conservator.

Any person named or acting as Executor may anytime pay or settle claims or debts they in their sole discretion find proper or helpful to pay, but I specifically say any secured debts including mortgages or liens on real property or vehicles should not be paid off unless parts of this Will specify it.

I give any person named or acting as Executor the fullest power and discretion allowed by state law, and I grant them all powers that may be conferred on Executors by state law.

Any person named or acting as Executor shall not be required to render and file annual accountings with respect to property or money including in relation to my Will or estate.

I authorize informal probate of my estate and Will and also administrative probate if any Executor chooses, and any Executor may act independently in all ways without supervision including from any court or judge.

I give any person named or acting as Executor authority to lease, sell, mortgage, convey, or retain property of mine in such manner and time they deem helpful or proper.

The residue includes lapsed or failed gifts, insurance paid to estate, inheritances owed me, and property I had a power of appointment or testamentary disposition over.

If in any place a Guardian of the Estate, Conservator, Administrator, Guardian of the Property, or any other fiduciary is needed for a child of mine or their estate or property, or for any other person, then I appoint for that the person named Executor above.

Any Executor, Personal Representative, Guardian, Administrator, Conservator, or fiduciary shall qualify and serve without bond, surety, security, or similar, including

despite their place of residence or lack of relationship to any state or country.

I name as Custodian under the Illinois Uniform Transfers to Minors Act or a similar law anywhere the person named in this Will as Guardian of the Estate or if they are unable to serve the person named Executor. An Executor using their sole discretion has power to at any time transfer money or property of a child or mine or any minor to this Custodian to serve under the Act until the minor is 18, and all without bond or any court action.

TESTATOR

IN WITNESS WHEREOF, I, _Susan Lee Maxwell_ , sign, publish, and declare this instrument as my Will, this __22nd__ day of __June__ , 20_22_ .

Susan Lee Maxwell
Testator signature

WITNESSES

We, the persons who sign below as witnesses to this Will, certify and attest that in presence of all witnesses on the date shown on this Will

that _Susan Lee Maxwell_ as Testator signed the Will and acknowledged it to be Testator's Will, and

that we witnesses at Testator's request and in presence of all other witnesses and Testator have signed our names as witnesses to the Will and attested the Will, and

that all the witnesses believed Testator to be of sound mind and memory at the time of signing the Will.

Nancy Ann Smith 24 Main St., Bond, IL 63882
Witness #1 signature   Witness #1 address

Pamela Bonnie Rooker 15 Roy St., Bond, IL 63881
Witness #2 signature   Witness #2 address

Sample Filled Out Form: Last Will and Testament (Standard)

LAST WILL AND TESTAMENT

I, <u>Henry James Ford</u>, of <u>Lake</u> County, Illinois, do revoke all prior Wills, Testaments, and Codicils, and do make, publish, and declare this to be my Will. When doing this I am of sound mind and under no duress or undue influence.

1. GIFTS. I give these gifts but to get a gift the recipient must survive the Testator, except as otherwise stated below.

I give <u>big oak table</u> to <u>Anne J. Wix.</u>

I give <u>$5,000</u> to <u>Loretta Marsha Switt</u> in the hope she will help her young daughter <u>Megan Kara Switt</u>.

I give <u>63 Ivy Road, Lundy, Illinois, 64087</u> to <u>Greta Olivia Fox.</u>

I give <u>all land in Troy, Illinois</u> to <u>Greta Olivia Fox.</u>

I give <u>9087 Wilderness Road, Bozeman, MT</u> to <u>James Tiberius Smith.</u>

I give <u>Bronze Roman Lamp</u> to <u>Anne Kilby</u> and <u>Kevin Kilby.</u>

I give <u>wedding ring</u> to <u>Ruth Jones.</u>

I give <u>all jewelry not given above</u> to <u>Kay Pidoski.</u>

I give <u>$7,281.35</u> to <u>Wanda Kay Zinski</u>.

I give <u>UBank account #8980443723</u> to <u>Joy Rundy a friend my sister knows about</u>.

I give <u>1998 Ford truck</u> to <u>John Smith my uncle.</u>

I give <u>a total of $50,000</u> to <u>Brian Peterson, Michael Peterson, and Mary Hart</u>.

I give <u>Wells Fargo acct ending in #8923</u> to <u>Lawrence Deer</u>.

I give <u>$1,000</u> to <u>that charity food kitchen on Smith Avenue in Kilby, Illinois.</u>

I give <u>all spare tires and tire rims</u> to <u>Victor Perez my mechanic</u>.

I give $6,000 in total   to   my cousin Carol Brown's children .

I give $500 each   to   each of my grandchildren   .

2. RESIDUE. I give the rest and residue and remainder of my estate, my property of any kind and nature, and anything I have an interest in (all of which is called the "residue"), so long as any such thing was not transferred by other Will provisions, as follows:
  a) to _____ Pamela Bonnie Ford my wife _____ who survive me with persons just named who survive me taking the share of non-survivors, then
  b) to my kids Ron Ford, Kevin Ford, Tina Ford, and Vera Hill and if any of those just named do not survive me their part goes to their lineal descendants, per stirpes.

3. ADMINISTRATION. I name and appoint   Pamela Bonnie Ford my wife   as Executor including for me, my Will, and my estate.

4. MISCELLANEOUS. The following applies to this Will and generally.
  Priority of Will gifts of the same type is based on the order they are written.
  The words "give" and "gift" also means a devise, bequest, grant, legacy, or similar.
  If gift or gift section mentions survival, survive, or surviving then survival is an absolute condition and anti-lapse laws or similar have no effect.
  In this document no unfilled part is a mistake and residue spaces may be left blank.
  Any failure to make gifts to family including children is intentional and not a mistake.
  No gift or transfer made during life reduces or offsets a Will gift unless during my life I expressly called it a "loan" or "advancement".
  Use of particular gender shall include other genders, reference to singular or plural shall be interchangeable, and "they" may be singular or plural.
  If context permits the terms Executor, Personal Representative, and Administrator shall be seen as interchangeable as if all were written, and if context permits Guardian of the Estate is interchangeable with Guardian of the Property and with Conservator.
  Any person named or acting as Executor may anytime pay or settle claims or debts they in their sole discretion find proper or helpful to pay, but I specifically say any secured debts including mortgages or liens on real property or vehicles should not be paid off unless parts of this Will specify it.
  I give any person named or acting as Executor the fullest power and discretion allowed by state law, and I grant them all powers that may be conferred on Executors by state law.
  Any person named or acting as Executor shall not be required to render and file annual accountings with respect to property or money including in relation to my Will or estate.

I authorize informal probate of my estate and Will and also administrative probate if any Executor chooses, and any Executor may act independently in all ways without supervision including from any court or judge.

I give any person named or acting as Executor authority to lease, sell, mortgage, convey, or retain property of mine in such manner and time they deem helpful or proper.

The residue includes lapsed or failed gifts, insurance paid to estate, inheritances owed me, and property I had a power of appointment or testamentary disposition over.

I name as Custodian under the Illinois Uniform Transfers to Minors Act or a similar law anywhere the person named in this Will as Guardian of the Estate or if they are unable to serve the person named Executor. An Executor using their sole discretion has power to at any time transfer money or property of a child or mine or any minor to this Custodian to serve under the Act until the minor is 18, and all without bond or any court action.

TESTATOR

IN WITNESS WHEREOF, I, *Henry James Ford* sign, publish, and declare this instrument as my Will, this *30th* day of *December,* 20*27*.

Henry James Ford
Testator signature

WITNESSES

We, the persons who sign below as witnesses to this Will, certify and attest that in presence of all witnesses on the date shown on this Will

that *Henry James Ford* as Testator signed the Will and acknowledged it to be Testator's Will, and

that we witnesses at Testator's request and in presence of all other witnesses and Testator have signed our names as witnesses to the Will and attested the Will, and

that all the witnesses believed Testator to be of sound mind and memory at the time of signing the Will.

Olivia Joy Pawlenty	87 Hastings Avenue, Buffalo, IL 63450
Witness #1	Address #1
Roy Felix Pawlenty	87 Hastings Avenue, Buffalo, IL 63450
Witness #2	Address #2

Sample Filled Out Form: Last Will and Testament (Guardians)

LAST WILL AND TESTAMENT

I, ___Ruth Ann Kent___, of __Cook__ County, Illinois, do revoke all prior Wills, Testaments, and Codicils, and do make, publish, and declare this to be my Will. When doing this I am of sound mind and under no duress or undue influence.

1. GIFTS. I give these gifts but to get a gift the recipient must survive the Testator, except as otherwise stated below.

I give silverware, copper bathtub, and boat to Ann Porter my niece.

I give 1987 Ford Truck and any other vehicles I own to Bill Porter my nephew.

I give $2,000 to Greg Best but if he fails to survive then his wife Jo Best.

I give $1,000 to the American Red Cross charity.

I give $2,250 to St. Joseph's my church.

I give $300 to Timmy Hart my paperboy.

I give a total of $10,000 50% to Abraham Daniel Walker, 40% to Amy Ann Hope, and 10% to Jennifer Kim Beaufort.

I give $1,300 and my cat Garfield to Sara Ham who I trust to care for him.

I give $5,000 to Juanita Chuzappa my Home Nurse but if she fails to survive me then to her children.

I give $100 to each of my first cousins.

I give $7,002.21 to Brenda Hill but if she fails to survive her son Eric Hill.

2. RESIDUE. I give the rest and residue and remainder of my estate, my property of any kind and nature, and anything I have an interest in (all of which is called the "residue"), so long as any such thing was not transferred by other Will provisions, as follows:

  a) to <u>Ken Rufus Kent my husband</u> who survive me with persons just named who survive me taking the share of non-survivors, then

  b) to <u>my young children Pamela Sue Kent and Adam David Kent</u> and if any of those just named do not survive me their part goes to their lineal descendants, per stirpes.

3. ADMINISTRATION. I name and appoint <u>Ken Rufus Kent my husband</u> as Executor including for me, my Will, and my estate.

4. GUARDIANS. I name and nominate <u>Helen Olivia Kent my sister</u> as Guardian of the Person of any child of mine or other person without full legal capacity. I name and nominate <u>Ken Rufus Kent my husband</u> as Guardian of the Estate of any minor child or infant of mine or other person without full legal capacity, and this person I name should be guardian for their money, property, and estate.

5. MISCELLANEOUS. The following applies to this Will and generally.

Priority of Will gifts of the same type is based on the order they are written.

The words "give" and "gift" also means a devise, bequest, grant, legacy, or similar.

If gift or gift section mentions survival, survive, or surviving then survival is an absolute condition and anti-lapse laws or similar have no effect.

In this document no unfilled part is a mistake and residue spaces may be left blank.

Any failure to make gifts to family including children is intentional and not a mistake.

No gift or transfer made during life reduces or offsets a Will gift unless during my life I expressly called it a "loan" or "advancement".

Use of particular gender shall include other genders, reference to singular or plural shall be interchangeable, and "they" may be singular or plural.

If context permits the terms Executor, Personal Representative, and Administrator shall be seen as interchangeable as if all were written, and if context permits Guardian of the Estate is interchangeable with Guardian of the Property and with Conservator.

Any person named or acting as Executor may anytime pay or settle claims or debts they in their sole discretion find proper or helpful to pay, but I specifically say any secured debts including mortgages or liens on real property or vehicles should not be paid off unless parts of this Will specify it.

I give any person named or acting as Executor the fullest power and discretion allowed by state law, and I grant them all powers that may be conferred on Executors by state law.

Any person named or acting as Executor shall not be required to render and file annual accountings with respect to property or money including in relation to my Will or estate.

I authorize informal probate of my estate and Will and also administrative probate if any Executor chooses, and any Executor may act independently in all ways without supervision including from any court or judge.

I give any person named or acting as Executor authority to lease, sell, mortgage, convey, or retain property of mine in such manner and time they deem helpful or proper.

The residue includes lapsed or failed gifts, insurance paid to estate, inheritances owed

me, and property I had a power of appointment or testamentary disposition over.

If in any place a Guardian of the Estate, Conservator, Administrator, Guardian of the Property, or any other fiduciary is needed for a child of mine or their estate or property, or for any other person, then I appoint for that the person named Executor above.

Any Executor, Personal Representative, Guardian, Administrator, Conservator, or fiduciary shall qualify and serve without bond, surety, security, or similar, including despite their place of residence or lack of relationship to any state or country.

I name as Custodian under the Illinois Uniform Transfers to Minors Act or a similar law anywhere the person named in this Will as Guardian of the Estate or if they are unable to serve the person named Executor. An Executor using their sole discretion has power to at any time transfer money or property of a child or mine or any minor to this Custodian to serve under the Act until the minor is 18, and all without bond or any court action.

TESTATOR

IN WITNESS WHEREOF, I, _Ruth Ann Kent_ did sign, publish, and declare this instrument as my Will, this _22nd_ day of _July_, 20_21_.

Ruth Ann Kent
Testator signature

WITNESSES

We, the persons who sign below as witnesses to this Will, certify and attest that in presence of all witnesses on the date shown on this Will

that _Ruth Ann Kent_ as Testator signed the Will and acknowledged it to be Testator's Will, and

that we witnesses at Testator's request and in presence of all other witnesses and Testator have signed our names as witnesses to the Will and attested the Will, and

that all the witnesses believed Testator to be of sound mind and memory at the time of signing the Will.

Susan Harriet Rogers   _87 Badger Road, Jacksonville, IL, 63307_
Witness #1   Address #1

Lucy Ann Pamway   _892 Franklin Street, Atlanta, GA 30301_
Witness #2   Address #2

**Sample Filled Out Form: Last Will and Testament (Standard)
with Simplified Residue Clause ***

LAST WILL AND TESTAMENT

I, **David Eric Smith**, a resident of **Cook** County, Illinois do revoke all prior Wills, Testaments, and Codicils, and do make, publish, and declare this to be my Will. When doing this I am of sound mind and under no duress or undue influence.

1. GIFTS. I give these gifts in this Will, but to get a gift in this section the recipient must survive me except as otherwise stated below.

I give _____ to _____.

I give _____ to _____.

I give _____ to _____.

I give _____ to _____.

I give _____ to _____.

I give _____ to _____.

I give _____ to _____.

I give _____ to _____.

I give _____ to _____.

I give _____ to _____.

2. RESIDUE. The rest and residue and remainder of my estate, my property of any kind and nature, and anything I have an interest in, I give to **Nancy Ann Smith and Pamela Bonnie Rooker my daughters who survive me**, and to lineal descendants per stirpes of a person just named who did not survive me.

3. ADMINISTRATION. I name and appoint **Nancy Ann Smith** my daughter as as Executor including for me, my Will, and my estate.

4. MISCELLANEOUS. The following applies to this Will and generally.

Priority of Will gifts of the same type is based on the order they are written.

The words "give" and "gift" also means a devise, bequest, grant, legacy, or similar.

If gift or gift section mentions survival, survive, or surviving then survival is an absolute condition and anti-lapse laws or similar have no effect.

In this document no unfilled part is a mistake and residue spaces may be left blank.

Any failure to make gifts to family including children is intentional and not a mistake.

No gift or transfer made during life reduces or offsets a Will gift unless during my life I expressly called it a "loan" or "advancement".

Use of particular gender shall include other genders, reference to singular or plural shall be interchangeable, and "they" may be singular or plural.

If context permits the terms Executor, Personal Representative, and Administrator shall be seen as interchangeable as if all were written, and if context permits Guardian of the Estate is interchangeable with Guardian of the Property and with Conservator.

Any person named or acting as Executor may anytime pay or settle claims or debts they in their sole discretion find proper or helpful to pay, but I specifically say any secured debts including mortgages or liens on real property or vehicles should not be paid off unless parts of this Will specify it.

I give any person named or acting as Executor the fullest power and discretion allowed by state law, and I grant them all powers that may be conferred on Executors by state law.

Any person named or acting as Executor shall not be required to render and file annual accountings with respect to property or money including in relation to my Will or estate.

I authorize informal probate of my estate and Will and also administrative probate if any Executor chooses, and any Executor may act independently in all ways without supervision including from any court or judge.

I give any person named or acting as Executor authority to lease, sell, mortgage, convey, or retain property of mine in such manner and time they deem helpful or proper.

The residue includes lapsed or failed gifts, insurance paid to estate, inheritances owed me, and property I had a power of appointment or testamentary disposition over.

If in any place a Guardian of the Estate, Conservator, Administrator, Guardian of the Property, or any other fiduciary is needed for a child of mine or their estate or property, or for any other person, then I appoint for that the person named Executor above.

Any Executor, Personal Representative, Guardian, Administrator, Conservator, or fiduciary shall qualify and serve without bond, surety, security, or similar, including despite their place of residence or lack of relationship to any state or country.

I name as Custodian under the Illinois Uniform Transfers to Minors Act or a similar law anywhere the person named in this Will as Guardian of the Estate or if they are unable

to serve the person named Executor. An Executor using their sole discretion has power to at any time transfer money or property of a child or mine or any minor to this Custodian to serve under the Act until the minor is 18, and all without bond or any court action.

TESTATOR

IN WITNESS WHEREOF, I, _David Eric Smith_ , sign, publish, and declare this instrument as my Will, this _21st_ day of _June_ , 20 _21_.

David Eric Smith
Testator signature

WITNESSES

We, the persons who sign below as witnesses to this Will, certify and attest that in presence of all witnesses on the date shown on this Will

that _David Eric Smith_ as Testator signed the Will and acknowledged it to be Testator's Will, and

that we witnesses at Testator's request and in presence of all other witnesses and Testator have signed our names as witnesses to the Will and attested the Will, and

that all the witnesses believed Testator to be of sound mind and memory at the time of signing the Will.

Nancy Ann Smith	204 Main Street, Buffalo, IL 61987
Witness signature	Witness address
Pamela Bonnie Rooker	83 River Road, Lakeville, IL 60428
Witness signature	Witness address

Sample Filled Out Form: Self-Proving Affidavit

SELF-PROVING AFFIDAVIT

STATE OF ILLINOIS)
) ss.
COUNTY OF ___Cook___)

We, the persons who sign below as witnesses, being first duly sworn, do hereby declare to the undersigned authority that

while we were present as witnesses to a Will being signed *David Eric Smith* did sign in the presence of both of us that Will as the Testator of it,

that this Testator signed that Will willingly as the Testator's free and voluntary act for the purposes set forth set forth in the document,

that each of us witnesses in the presence of this Testator and in the presence of each other signed as a witness to that Will, and

that to the best of our knowledge the Testator was at the time of signing of that Will of sound mind and memory and under no constraint or undue influence.

Nancy Ann Smith   204 Main Street, Buffalo, IL 61987
Witness signature   Witness address

Pamela Bonnie Rooker   83 River Road, Lakeville, IL 60428
Witness signature   Witness address

NOTARY OR OFFICER

Signed and sworn to before me on this *21st* day of *June*, 20 *21* by *Nancy Ann Smith* and *Pamela Bonnie Rooker* witnesses.

(Seal)

```
OFFICIAL SEAL
JOHN DODD
NOTARY PUBLIC, STATE OF ILLINOIS
My Commission Expires April 28, 2025
```

John Dodd
Notary Public, State of Illinois

www.ingramcontent.com/pod-product-compliance
Lightning Source LLC
Chambersburg PA
CBHW060416220526
45465CB00008B/2900